LIVING THE ANABAPTIST STORY

A Guide to Early Beginnings with Questions for Today

LISA D. WEAVER and J. DENNY WEAVER

Illustration and design by
Judith Rempel Smucker

Cascadia

Publishing House
Telford, Pennsylvania

Cascadia Publishing House LLC orders, information, reprint permissions:
contact@cascadiapublishinghouse.com
1-215-723-9125
126 Klingerman Road, Telford PA 18969
www.CascadiaPublishingHouse.com

Living the Anabaptist Story
Copyright © 2015 by Cascadia Publishing House
a division of Cascadia Publishing House LLC, Telford, PA 18969
All rights reserved.
Library of Congress Catalog Number: 2015027869
ISBN-13: 978-1-68027-004-4
Book and cover design by Judith Rempel Smucker

All Bible quotations are used by permission, all rights reserved and, unless otherwise
noted, are from *The New Revised Standard Version of the Bible*, copyright 1989,
by the Division of Christian Education of the National Council of the Churches of Christ in
the USA.

Library of Congress Cataloguing-in-Publication Data
Weaver, Lisa D., author.
Living the Anabaptist story : a guide to early beginnings with questions for today / by Lisa
D. Weaver and J. Denny Weaver ; Illustrations and design by Judith Rempel Smucker.
     pages cmg
Includes bibliographical references and index.
Summary: "This accessible history tells the story of how adult Christians of the 1500s
shaped the Anabaptist believers church tradition, which lives on today and can be joined
by any who identify with Anabaptist understandings of following Christ"— Provided by
publisher.
ISBN 978-1-68027-004-4 (8 x 8 trade pbk. with full-color illustrations : alk. paper)
 1. Anabaptists—History—Juvenile literature. 2. Anabaptists—North America—Juvenile
literature. I. Weaver, J. Denny, 1941- author. II. Smucker, Judith Rempel, 1955- illustrator.
III. Title.

 BX4931.3.W44 2015
 284'.309—dc23

2015027869

22 21 20 11 19 18 17 16 15   10 9 8 7 6 5 4 3 2 1

*To all
who carry the story
forward*

Therefore, since we are surrounded
by so great a cloud of witnesses,
let us also lay aside every weight and
the sin that clings so closely,
and let us run with perseverance the race
that is set before us, looking to Jesus
the pioneer and perfecter of our faith.

Hebrews 12:1-2a

Table of Contents

Map of Anabaptist Locations in 1500s Europe
(modern national boundaries)

BALTIC SEA

NORTH SEA

Emden •

Wüstenfelde •

Danzig/Gdansk •

VISTULA RIVER DELTA

Witmarsum • ← *FRIESLAND*

NETHERLANDS

Amsterdam •

GERMANY

Münster •

RHINE RIVER

ODER RIVER

POLAND/PRUSSIA

VISTULA RIVER

Wittenberg •

Schwarzenau
(Brethren in 1700s)

Prague •

CZECH REPUBLIC

MORAVIA

Austerlitz/Auspitz/Rossitz •

Nikolsburg •

Strasbourg •

DANUBE RIVER

Passau •

FRANCE

ALSACE

Schleitheim •

Basel •

Zurich •

Bern •

SWITZERLAND

AUSTRIA

• Münichau Castle

TYROL **Innsbruck** •

TYROL

ITALY

In the 1500s Anabaptism originated in Europe in three areas—Switzerland, The Netherlands, and the South German region (now Germany, Austria, Moravia/Czech Republic).

Introduction

In its most basic sense, the word Anabaptist means "one who is baptized again." In the sixteenth century, this name was given to individuals who chose to be baptized as adults after having been baptized as infants. Baptism marked the choice to leave the established state church and join a new church of adult believers.

In the twenty-first century, Anabaptism has taken on an identity that means more than simply baptism as an adult. Anabaptists today hold dear the values of nonviolence and pacifism, the example of Jesus as a life model, and a conscious effort to live within a faith community. Many (but not all) Anabaptist leaders of the the sixteenth century also cherished these values, and it is this peaceful, Christ-centered legacy that carries forward into the twenty-first century. It is significant to note that the names held by Anabaptist denominations today come from our pacifist ancestors: Mennonites (Menno Simons), Hutterites (Jacob Hutter), and Amish (Jakob Ammann, from the seventeenth century). As well, the first minister of the Brethren movement (Alexander Mack) carried the conviction of nonviolence.

The stories contained within these pages are not the property of a single group of people, determined by citizenship or family name. Rather, the stories of the first Anabaptists belong to all Anabaptist communities of the present time. For indeed, that is a hallmark of Anabaptism—that an adult believer chooses to enter a faith community, and chooses to identify as a follower of Christ. Anyone can claim the Anabaptist story. Therefore, we invite you to explore the following pages and consider where you would like to place yourself in the future we are creating today.

Lisa Weaver

J. Denny Weaver

explore the past

act in the present

shape the future

Anabaptist Paths

1500s	Switzerland		The Netherlands/Holland
1600s	Mennonites	Amish	Mennonites to Poland/Prussia
1700s	to U.S. + Canada	to U.S. + Canada	to Russia
1800s	Old Order Mennonites	Change-minded Mennonites, Amish, Brethren in Christ	Old Order Amish	to Canada + U.S.
1900s				to Canada + Latin America
2000s	**Your Congregation of Believers**		

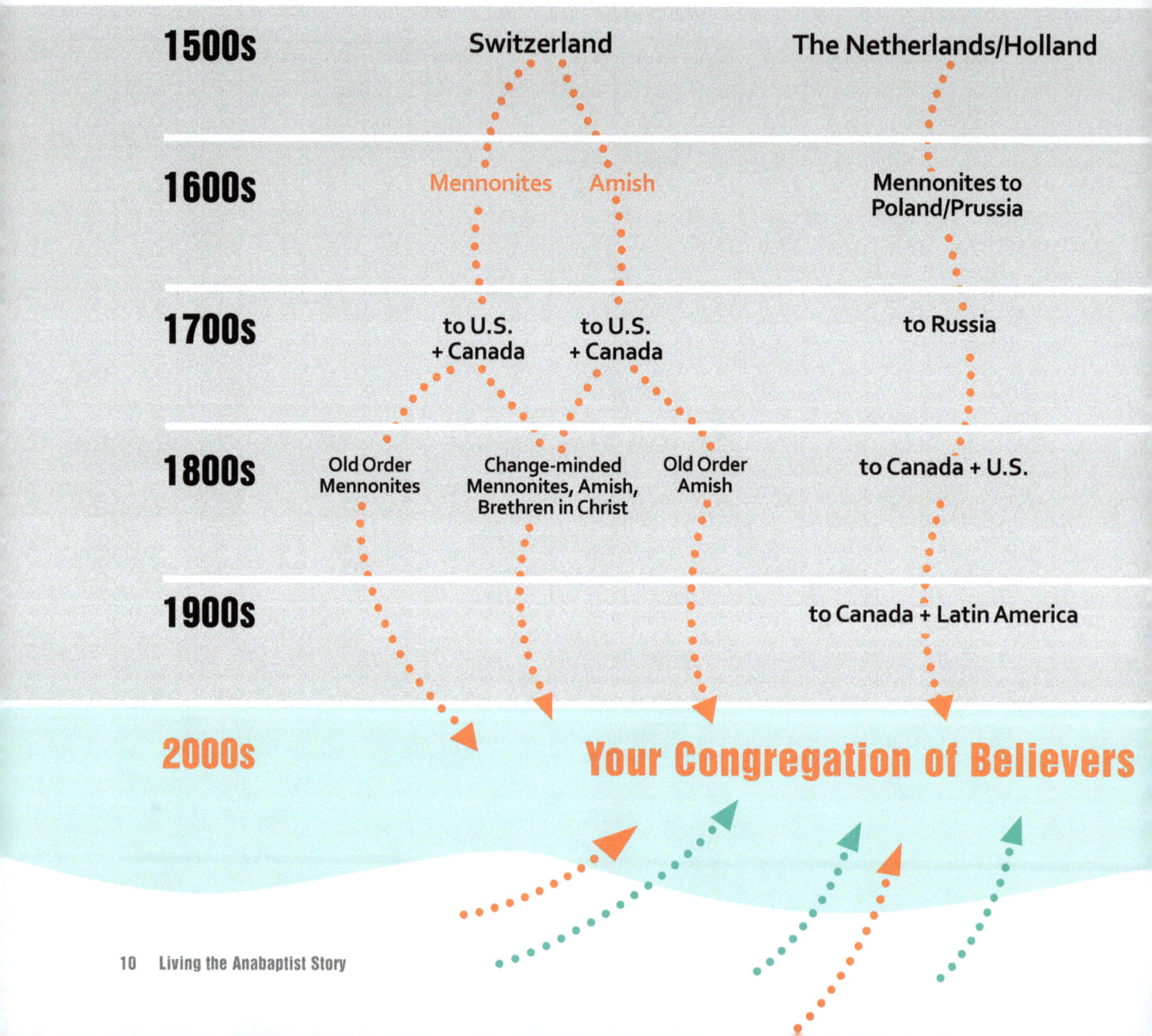

# of European Origins

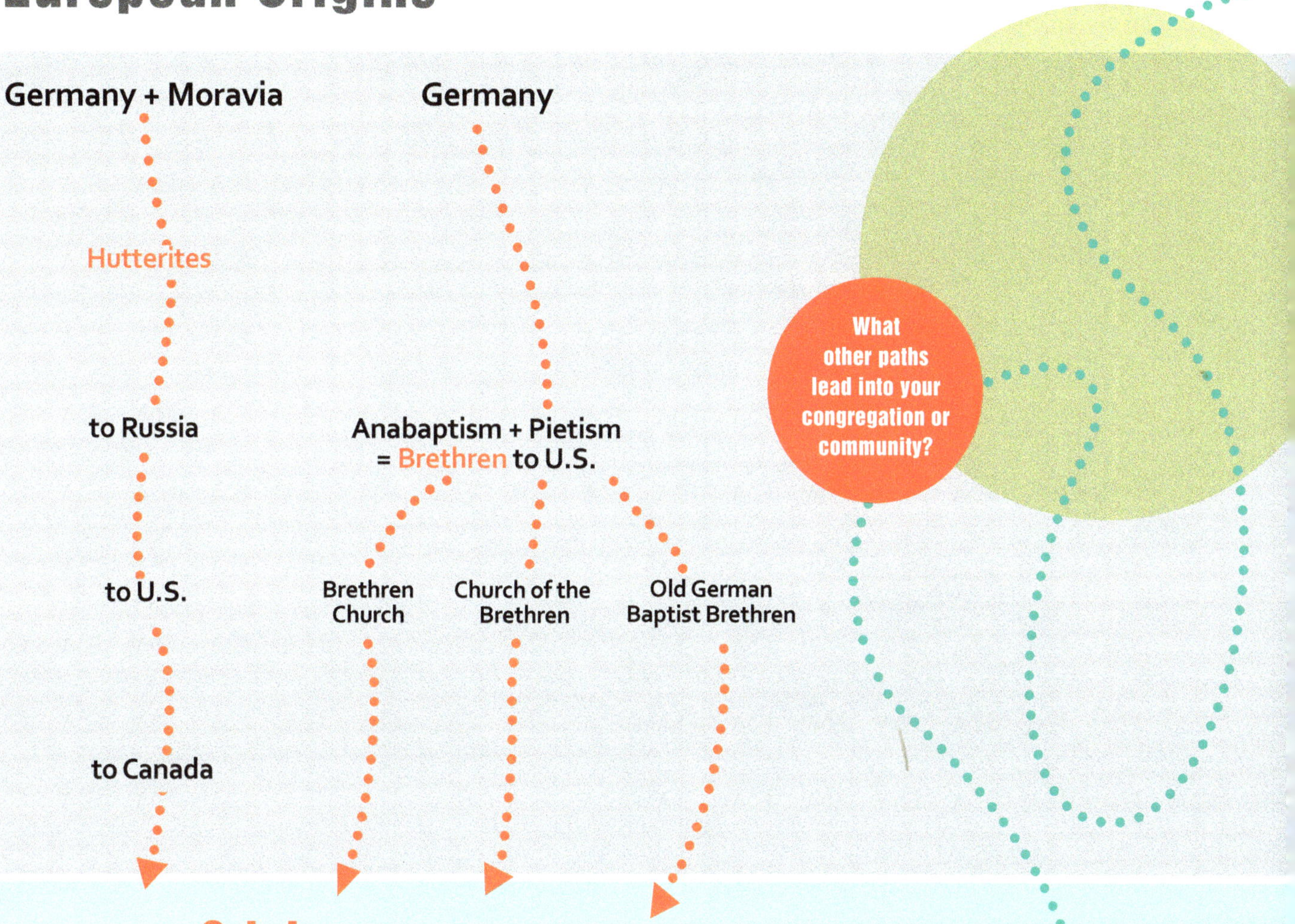

Germany + Moravia

Germany

Hutterites

to Russia

Anabaptism + Pietism
= Brethren to U.S.

to U.S.

Brethren
Church

Church of the
Brethren

Old German
Baptist Brethren

to Canada

What other paths lead into your congregation or community?

from many Origins

The replica statue of Holy Roman Emperor Charlemagne (742-814) stands on the south tower of Zurich's *Grossmünster* church. The imperial sword and imperial scepter symbolize the military and civil authority that was used to suppress the early Anabaptist movement.

The Protestant Reformation

To study the Anabaptists, it is helpful to look first at a wider movement called the Reformation of the Sixteenth Century. Martin Luther, an Augustinian monk and professor at Wittenberg University, is credited with beginning this movement. His actions challenged the established church, which at that time was recognized as the only church.

MARTIN LUTHER

On October 31, 1517, Martin Luther posted his 95 Theses in the city of Wittenberg, Germany. Before the age of the radio, television, and the Internet, posting papers was one way that a person could make public his or her views on a given subject. The 95 Theses was a document that Luther wrote, listing the concerns that he had with the church practice of selling indulgences. Luther was reacting to a specific indulgence being offered by a traveling indulgence seller near the city of Wittenberg.

INDULGENCES

An indulgence was a contract that an individual could buy to shorten the time a person would spend in purgatory. It was believed that most people would spend long periods of time—even hundreds of years—in purgatory before moving on to heaven. Purgatory was the place where the penalty of sin was purged, or gotten rid of. Purgatory was believed to be the most likely destination after death, the other two possibilities being heaven and hell. It was taught that only saints could go directly to heaven, and sinners without remorse would go to hell.

Buyers bought indulgences for themselves or for loved ones in order to shorten the time one would have to spend in purgatory. Even poor people would scrape together what little money they had to buy an indulgence. Johann Tetzel was the traveling indulgence seller near Wittenberg, whose

The sale of indulgences was a widespread practice of the church in the 1500s, here shown in a woodcut of that century. In addition to their theological purpose, indulgence income was used to fund projects of the Pope. Martin Luther and others disputed the theology of indulgences and resented the drain on the resources of the people.

indulgence Martin Luther protested. It was like a "free pass" out of purgatory. Pope Leo X had authorized the sale of this indulgence. Profits from indulgence sales went to various church projects.

Luther protested the idea of a free pass. Soon after publishing this opinion, he expanded the statement to say that an indulgence was not necessary at all to receive forgiveness of sin. Rather, the grace of God is available to a repentant heart without an indulgence.

LUTHER'S REFORM MOVEMENT

Eventually Luther outlined an orderly plan to reform the church.

This meant that he did not want to leave the church, but he wanted the church to change in some way. The major points that Luther talked about were communion, the priesthood of all believers, and the belief that people are saved by faith and not by doing works or paying penalties.

Within a few years, Luther's reform movement affected much of Europe. When the religious dimensions of the movement are talked about, it is referred to as the Protestant Reformation. When the movement is seen to affect not only religion but also social, economic, and political conditions, it is referred to as the Reformation of the Sixteenth Century.

The Reformation was well underway when the Anabaptists entered the scene. The first Anabaptists (as defined by the first adult baptisms) were individuals who eventually established a separate church rather than reform the existing one. Anabaptists thought that the reform movements—those led by Luther, Ulrich Zwingli, and John Calvin—had not gone far enough. Simply put, Anabaptists desired to remove themselves altogether from the established church and begin a new church. It is helpful, therefore, to clarify what is meant by the established church of the sixteenth century.

ESTABLISHED CHURCH (STATE CHURCH)

Established church refers to the church that is formed by, connected to, and protected by the civil government of a region. In modern language this could be called a state church. In other words, anyone living in sixteenth-century Europe was a member of the church simply by being born there. Prior to the Reformation, the church was simply called "the church," because there was no other church in Western Europe from which to distinguish it. The head of the church was the pope, who lived in Rome. Local parishes were a part of this larger church system. After other churches came into existence, this original established church came to be known as the Catholic Church.

definition

REFORMED CHURCH
A reformed church was one that did not separate itself from the established church system but desired to reform (or change) itself, either in theology or practice.

Martin Luther (1483-1546) was a monk in Germany who eventually decided to leave monastic life. He married Katharina von Bora in 1525. Luther helped lead the Protestant Reformation, but he eventually opposed the radical reforms advocated by the Anabaptists. Luther translated the Bible into German.

What movements are occurring in your congregation or community today?

THE ANABAPTIST MOVEMENT

Anabaptist is a term used for people who are baptized as adults. It specifically means baptized again, or rebaptized. Anabaptists sought to separate themselves completely from the established church. Because it had been official policy for more than a thousand years to baptize all infants into the established church, rejecting infant baptism and asking for adult baptism was no small matter. In fact, it was a crime against civil law. Those identified as Anabaptists faced grave danger; they could be imprisoned, tortured, or even killed. The term *Anabaptist* was originally a negative term, used by those who chased down and arrested Anabaptists. Anabaptists often met in secret, holding Bible studies in homes, woods, or caves.

Anabaptism emerged in three major geographical areas in the sixteenth century. Swiss Anabaptists were from Switzerland. The South German-Moravian Anabaptist story centered in southern Germany and Moravia. Dutch Anabaptists were from the Netherlands, a region referred to as the Low Countries.

Social issues contributed to the rise of Anabaptism. Common and working class people chafed under both civil and religious rule. Civil rulers created economic systems that disadvantaged the common people and then were willing to use violence to silence protesters. An example is the massacre of 6000 peasants on May 15, 1525, at Frankenhausen which ended a rebellion called the Peasants War.

Commoners had also come to resent religious authorities because of

definition

BELIEVERS CHURCH
The believers church is a community of individuals who choose to follow Jesus, and be a part of the church that forms around Jesus. Membership into this community is marked by believers baptism. In the sixteenth century, Anabaptists formed the believers church as an alternative to the church that was established by the city or state government.

definition

FREE CHURCH
Since a believers church is free of—meaning, independent from—the established church, the believers church can also be called the free church.

oppressive taxation, the buying and selling of church offices, and the selling of indulgences. Because Anabaptists were creating a new community separate from the civil and religious authorities, some who were dissatisfied with the current way society operated were drawn to the Anabaptist movement. The practices of adult baptism, lay leadership, and the reading and discussing of scripture by all members of the community were empowering to commoners who were feeling oppressed by the ruling class.

There were likewise individuals who came to the Anabaptist movement from ruling class, educated, or priestly backgrounds. These individuals likewise found meaning in the centrality of the scriptures, the absence of hierarchy, and life within an intentional community.

The shared Anabaptist outlook was based on an understanding of the church as a separate, alternative community of adult believers. Discipleship to Jesus (using the life and teachings of Jesus as a norm) provided structure for this new society. Therefore scriptures, particularly the New Testament, were central to the life of the church.

BAPTISM

Baptism is a religious practice involving water. It may involve the sprinkling or pouring of water on an individual's head. Baptism may also be practiced by total immersion in water.

Infant baptism

The established church of the sixteenth century practiced infant baptism. Since all members of a territory were considered to be part of the church, it was expected that all infants would be baptized. The act of baptizing drew the baby into the state church.

Infant baptism involved the belief that every human inherited original sin, which needed to be removed by the act of baptism. Original sin is supposedly the sin committed by Adam and Eve in the Garden of Eden, and passed down through all of humankind.

Believers baptism (adult baptism)

Anabaptists rejected the idea of infant baptism. Anabaptists believed that a person ought to choose to belong to a church rather than be born into it. Anabaptists created a new church, independent of civil authorities. Adult baptism marked the choice to join the church. Balthasar Hubmaier, an Anabaptist pastor from the town of Waldshut (near Zurich) wrote the first major paper on adult baptism.

The German Peasants' War (1524-1525) was a rebellion that ended with the violent slaughter of thousands of peasants and victory for the existing nobility. This image from 1525 shows the peasants (left) lined up against the soldiers (right) of the nobility and rulers.

Describe a baptism you have witnessed.

Anabaptists rejected the idea that an unbaptized infant was automatically damned to hell because of original sin. Instead, Anabaptists believed that children were not born sinful and that individuals were only responsible for their actions once they reached the age of accountability.

Since the state church was also the framework for civil society, it was threatening to civil authorities for citizens to join a church unconnected to the state. When sixteenth-century Anabaptists chose not to baptize their newborn babies or when adults asked for believers baptism, they were at risk for persecution. Anabaptists could be arrested, imprisoned, tortured, or put to death.

This adult baptism took place in the early 1900s in the Ginqa River in Zimbabwe. In 2012 there were more than 46,000 members of the Brethren in Christ church (an Anabaptist group) in 288 congregations in Zimbabwe.

In Zurich between 1523 and 1525 a series of public meetings, called disputations, were held. Questions discussed included: Who has authority to carry out church reform? Should infants be baptized? At the November 1525 disputation, the city council, with Zwingli's support, decided that adult baptism, recently practiced by Anabaptists, was illegal. Anabaptists could be punished by life in prison or death.

Ulrich Zwingli (1481-1531) became the first leader of the Swiss Reformed Church in Canton Zurich. His earliest circle of followers in Zurich city included people who would later break with him and lead the Anabaptist movement.

The First Anabaptists

Ulrich Zwingli was a *Leutpriester* (people's priest) at the *Grossmünster*, the main church of Zurich, Switzerland. As a leading church reformer, Zwingli was aware of Martin Luther's beginning reform work.

When Zwingli arrived in Zurich in 1518, he started immediately with reform measures. For example, he began what was then the unusual practice of preaching to his congregation directly from the New Testament, starting with Matthew. Prior to this, priests would have followed the scriptures prescribed by the church year. Also as part of his reform measures, Zwingli removed icons (statues) from the church and painted over images in the *Grossmünster*.

In March of 1522, Zwingli was present when a deliberate, public act of challenge to the established church took place. He was among those gathered in a print shop owned by a man named Christoph Froschauer. The print shop had a big job to complete. When the work was finally done, Froschauer got out sausage to share with those who were helping him. However, since the church forbid anyone to eat meat during the season of Lent, this was a violation of church law. Though Zwingli did not eat the sausage himself, he did not stop anyone else from doing so. When the story of the sausage-eating became public, Zwingli could have confessed the wrongdoing and asked for forgiveness. Instead, he preached a sermon in the *Grossmünster* defending the eating of meat during Lent. Actions such as this caused Zwingli to be known as a church reformer— someone who was a part of the church but wanted to change church practices or understandings.

When, and with whom, do you read the Bible?

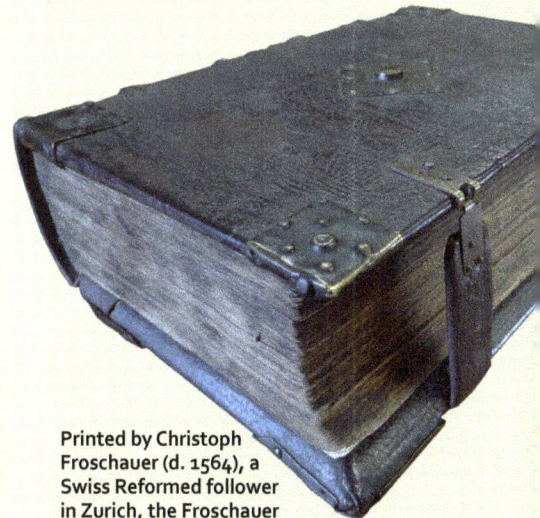

Printed by Christoph Froschauer (d. 1564), a Swiss Reformed follower in Zurich, the Froschauer Bible was a translation of the Bible into a form of German that the Swiss could understand better. The earliest editions (especially 1525) became a favorite of the Swiss Anabaptists, which they had reprinted many times. They often brought them as they fled Switzerland, as this one was brought to Germany in the 1670s. In the later 1500s and 1600s it was against the law in Canton Bern to possess the earlier editions, and authorities used this law to identify and punish Anabaptists.

ANDREAS CASTELBERGER

Andreas Castelberger was a traveling bookseller from Chur who eventually settled in Zurich and opened a bookstore. Following the example of his pastor Ulrich Zwingli, Castelberger started a Bible study group in 1522 that read the Greek New Testament, published by Desiderius Erasmus in 1516.

FELIX MANTZ AND CONRAD GREBEL

Conrad Grebel and Felix Mantz were among the young men who attended the Bible study led by Andreas Castelberger. Though originally enthusiastic supporters of the reform efforts led by Ulrich Zwingli, Mantz and Grebel eventually grew frustrated with what they thought was the slow pace and reluctance of Zwingli to make real change. Grebel came to believe that Zwingli was not allowing scripture (and the teachings found within) to be the authority for reform. Grebel said that Zwingli was putting his faith in the governance of the city council of Zurich. The disagreement between Zwingli and these more radical reformers could be seen in the disputations (public meetings) held between 1523 and 1525.

DISPUTATIONS IN ZURICH

In the era of the Reformation, public disputations could vary in format but had the characteristics of a debate or a modern-day hearing in which a program is laid out and interested parties can register protests. Supposedly, a disputation was a safe place in which to voice complaints or opinions. However, in sixteenth-century Europe, registering an opposing opinion was sometimes cause for arrest.

There were four major disputations in Zurich, Switzerland, related to the Anabaptist story. In each of these disputations, Ulrich Zwingli (lead pastor at the Grossmünster) laid out his reform measures for the church.

January 1523

This disputation discussed the authority for reforming the church. Zwingli proposed that the Bible should be the basis, or authority, for reformation. Though twenty-first-century Christians may not perceive a call for Bible-reading as a radical position, sixteenth-century Europe considered this a major challenge to the authority of the Pope and the Roman hierarchy; when individuals read and interpreted the Bible for themselves, it opened the possibility that a person might reach and then promote a different view than the Pope.

How are issues discussed, and decisions made in your church or community today?

In Zurich this plaque marks the location where Conrad Grebel lived from 1508 to 1514 and from 1520 to 1525. In 1525 Grebel, Felix Mantz, and others in the Swiss Anabaptist movement definitively broke with Zwingli's Swiss Reformed Church.

IN·DIESEM·HAUSE·WOHNTE 1508–1514 UND 1520–1525 KONRAD GREBEL DER·ZUSAMMEN·MIT·FELIX MANZ DAS·TÄUFERTUM·BEGRÜNDETE

The city council approved Zwingli's proposal for reform and confirmed Zwingli as head of the church in Zurich. With this move, the city council rejected the authority of the Pope, and the church in Zurich officially became a reforming church. In other words, it remained the church established by the city government but identified itself as being reform-minded.

October 1523

This October disputation in Zurich was on the understanding of the mass and the use of icons in churches. The disputation resulted in clear statements that neither the mass as practiced nor the presence of icons had any support in the Bible. When Grebel asked for immediate instructions on carrying out reforms, Zwingli replied that it would be up to the city council to decide how and when reforms would take place. Grebel was bitterly disappointed. Zwingli's position was that the city council should decide the strategy for reform so that it could be carried out without offending the populace. To Grebel, this seemed as if Zwingli was now standing in the way of reform and merely transferring power from the pope to the city council. This was the beginning of the split between Zwingli and the radicals who would soon become the first Anabaptists.

January 1525

In this disputation, Zwingli defended the long-standing tradition of infant baptism. Grebel and others protested the defense of infant baptism, but the council approved Zwingli's measure. It was immediately after this January 17 ruling that Grebel, George Blaurack, Felix Mantz, and others organized the first adult baptisms. The baptisms were a direct response, and an open challenge, to Zwingli and the city council.

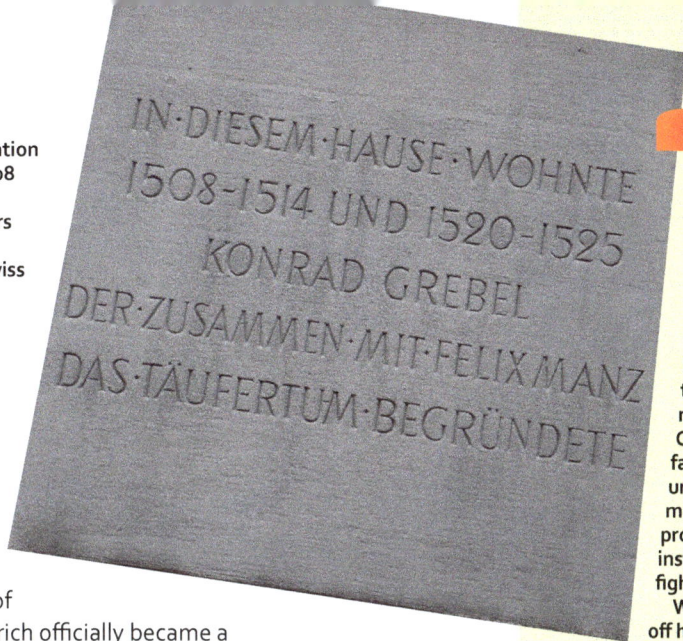

November 1525

This second disputation on baptism took place in Zurich. It confirmed the city council rulings of the first baptismal disputation. This ruling confirmed that city officials could arrest those who practiced adult baptism.

ANNA AND FELIX MANTZ

The first adult baptisms took place between the January and November disputations in Zurich. The baptisms took place in the home of Anna Mantz (mother to Felix) on January 21, 1525. Anna lived in Zurich, just down the street from the *Grossmünster*. George Blaurock, a former priest at Chur, requested baptism from Grebel. Then Blaurock baptized the rest of those present. Anna and Felix Mantz were among those rebaptized.

On October 8, 1525, Blaurock, Grebel, and Felix Mantz were arrested for Anabaptist activity. After the November 1525 disputation which confirmed that adult baptism was indeed illegal, they were given life terms in prison. However, on March 21, 1526, they escaped from prison by means of a rope through an unlocked window.

Felix Mantz was eventually arrested again for continued Anabaptist activity. On January 5, 1527, he was led to the Limmat River in Zurich to be drowned for the crime of being an Anabaptist. His mother Anna stood on the banks of the river and watched. She called out to him, urging him to be steadfast in his beliefs. Feliz Mantz was the first Anabaptist martyr in Zurich.

George Blaurock was later arrested in the South Tyrol Basin and burned at the stake in July 1529.

"To speak is not pleasant for me, nor is it easy, for he [Zwingli] has already so often overwhelmed me with so much speaking that I was not able to answer or could not find room to answer because of his long speeches." *Felix Mantz, explaining why he was putting his defense of adult baptism into writing.*

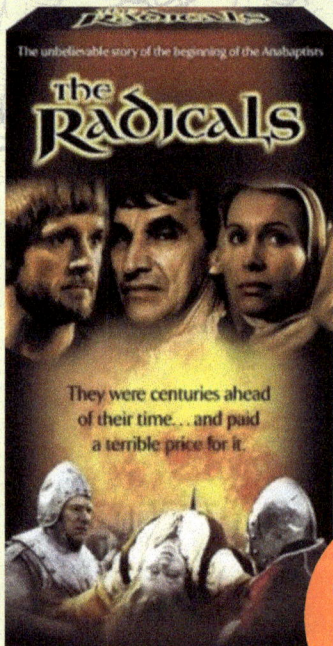

Produced in 1990, *The Radicals* is a video that tells the story of the early Swiss Anabaptists.

What is the religious diversity present in your community today?

This drawing of the 1600s shows Anabaptist George Blaurock being bound and whipped in 1525 as he was driven out of Zurich due to his religious beliefs.

This drawing of the 1600s depicts Felix Mantz being executed by drowning on January 5, 1527, in the Limmat River in Zurich. He was the first Anabaptist martyr in Zurich. In 2004 the Zurich city council took an unprecedented step of placing a plaque near the spot where Mantz was martyred. The English translation of the inscription reads: "Here in the middle of the Limmat River from a fishing platform, Felix Manz and five other Anabaptists were drowned between 1527 and 1532 during the Reformation. The last Anabaptist executed in Zurich was Hans Landis in 1614." Representatives of the Swiss Reformed Church asked for forgiveness for these past deeds, an important step in reconciliation between Mennonites and Reformed.

Zurich authorities, armed with guns and/or clubs, are overtaking a secret meeting of Anabaptists in the forest near Altstetten. This drawing from the 1600s shows the violent force used against the Anabaptists in Switzerland. Facing such sustained opposition, Anabaptists in Europe developed their church and their cultural life in a separated and tightly-knit way.

Early Anabaptist Thought and Practice

THE SCHLEITHEIM ARTICLES

On February 24, 1527, a small group of Anabaptists met in Schleitheim, Switzerland. This meeting produced the Schleitheim Articles. This document (also called the Schleitheim Confession), was the first Anabaptist statement that described a free church—a church independent from civil or governmental authorities. Michael Sattler, who attended the meetings, was its major author.

The Schleitheim Articles came to define Swiss Anabaptism. There are seven sections to the document.

Section I: Adult baptism
Those who choose to walk in the resurrection of Jesus Christ will be baptized.

Section II: Church discipline
A ban will be enacted upon any member of the community who breaks the rules of the community.

Section III: Lord's Supper
To participate in the symbolic event of the Lord's Supper, a person must belong to the united body of Christ.

Section IV: Separation from civil authority
The church will be separate from state churches and unhealthy social practices such as frequenting taverns.

Section V: Ministers
Ministers will be selected from within the congregation.

Title page of a 1659 mandate against Anabaptists from Canton Bern, Switzerland, one of many official acts passed over the years in an attempt to eradicate them from Bern. In contrast, Swiss Anabaptists wrote the Schleitheim Articles, which defined a separation between the church and civil authorities.

Which of these practices are visible in your congregation or community today?

25

MICHAEL SATTLER (d. 1527)
Michael Sattler was educated as a Catholic brother and served in the Black Forest Monastery of Saint Peter in southern Germany. Sattler's exact path to Anabaptism is not known, but he appears in Zurich by June 1526 as an Anabaptist. It is possible that Sattler's decision to leave the monastery was influenced by the occupation of Saint Peter's on May 12, 1525, by a troop of peasants from the Peasants Revolt.

In 1526 and 1527, Sattler spent time in both Zurich and Strasbourg. In Strasbourg, Sattler interacted with other Anabaptists and also engaged in discussion with Reformed pastors Martin Bucer and Wolfgang Capito. When he left Strasbourg, he wrote a cordial letter explaining his theological differences with Bucer and Capito.

Following his participation in the Schleitheim meetings, Sattler went on to pastor the Anabaptist congregation at Horb, South Germany. However, he was soon arrested by Austrian authorities, who were carrying out the oppressive policies of Archduke Ferdinand. Ferdinand sought to eradicate (remove, or kill) all Anabaptists from his political lands.

Sattler was tried on May 17-18, 1527. He was cruelly tortured, and then burned at the stake on May 20 by the Neckar River at Rottenberg. Wolfgang Capito, one of the reform church pastors at Strasbourg wrote to the Rottenberg mayor and council. Capito defended the strong moral character of Sattler and decried his death. Martin Bucer likewise defended the character of Sattler in a booklet that he wrote.

Sattler's wife, Margueretha, was drowned in the Neckar River two days after his death.

Section VI: Rejection of the Sword
The use of the sword is outside the perfection of Christ but allowed to civil authorities.

Section VII: Refusal to swear civil oaths.
Christians will refuse to use civil oaths.

PILGRAM MARPECK

Pilgram Marpeck was born about 1495 and grew up in the city of Rattenberg, in Austrian territory. His family was wealthy and politically important. Marpeck's father served on the outer and inner councils of the city and also served a term as mayor. At age eighteen, Marpeck was made an assistant administrator of a local hospital and then was a member of the city council and served a term as mayor in 1522. In April 1525 he was appointed to the important office of superintendent of mines; this office governed the entire mining industry.

As a city employee, Marpeck was expected to assist in the arrest of Anabaptists. He was, however, greatly disturbed when Anabaptists Hans Schlaffer and Lienhard Schiemer were arrested and executed. Following this event, Marpeck resigned his position as mine inspector and left Rattenberg.

His wife Sophia had just died. Leaving Rattenberg meant abandoning significant property, wealth, and his wife's grave.

Marpeck spent a few months in Krumau in southern Germany, where there were Anabaptist refugees from Rattenberg. Refugees were also arriving from Austerlitz. Among these was Anna, who became his wife. In September 1528 Marpeck and Anna moved to Strasbourg, where Marpeck bought citizenship and was hired as the city water and fuel engineer. Marpeck soon became leader of the Anabaptist community in Strasbourg. He lived in and around Strasbourg until he was finally expelled from the city in January 1532 because of his Anabaptist activities.

In 1544 Marpeck moved to Augsburg. Again he worked as a city engineer, this time in charge of the city's forests and water supply. Along with periods of intermittent harassment, he functioned as a leader of the Anabaptist community in Augsburg. He was an important leader of a network of congregations connected to the Anabaptist community at Austerlitz. In recent years, this network has been called the Marpeck circle. In Anabaptist churches of the twenty-first century, this network would be similar to a regional conference.

Marpeck died of natural causes in 1556.

Letters and books

Marpeck's many writings have been preserved in letters and books. An important element of Marpeck's thought was his complete rejection of the sword. Specifically, Marpeck was critical of the Lutheran princes who were developing a coalition of Protestant princes to fight against Catholic princes and the Catholic Emperor. Marpeck also outlined the idea that the church is independent of civil authority and stressed the significance of the Sermon on the Mount as a model for daily life. Marpeck's correspondence with Swiss Anabaptists revealed his opinion that they wrongly held to an overly legalistic interpretation of the Bible—emphasizing rules at the expense of loving, faithful actions. Marpeck also challenged the view of Spiritualists, whom he thought did not take seriously the importance of visible ceremonies of baptism and the Lord's supper, or acknowledge the humanity of Christ.

THE LORD'S SUPPER

The Lord's Supper is the last meal that Jesus shared with his disciples before he was crucified on the cross. This meal is described in Matthew 26:26-29, Mark 14:22-25, Luke 22:14-23, and I Corinthians 11:23-26 of the New Testament.

The Lord's Supper can also refer to the ritual meal of worship. In this faith

Pilgram Marpeck (ca. 1495-1556), important Anabaptist leader in Germany, lived in various locations, including Strasbourg. He left many writings, which stress a complete rejection of violence, the idea that the Sermon on the Mount is a model for daily life, and an emphasis on the humanity of Jesus Christ. This is an artist's idea of how Marpeck may have appeared.

Strasbourg

Strasbourg was a city on the border of Germany and France; today, it is in France. Martin Bucer and Wolfgang Capito were the reform leaders of the established church in Strasbourg. Because of their relatively tolerant policy towards Anabaptists, many Anabaptists spent time in Strasbourg.

practice, Christians share bread, drink juice or wine, and recall the words of Jesus at the Last Supper. Also called communion, this practice is followed by Christians around the world. In some traditions, communion is referred to as the Eucharist.

There are many early and modern interpretations of the practice of communion. The Catholic Church teaches that the bread and wine turn into the actual body and blood of Jesus. Martin Luther of the Protestant Reformation believed that the bread remained bread and the wine remained wine but that the body and blood of Jesus were still present in the bread and wine. This view is called belief in the real presence.

Anabaptists adopted the teaching of reform minister Ulrich Zwingli of Zurich. Zwingli said that the bread and wine could not be the body and blood of Jesus because Jesus was in heaven sitting at the right hand of God. Zwingli believed that the bread stayed bread and the wine stayed wine. The elements of communion were symbols of Jesus' body and blood. Modern Anabaptists hold this belief today.

PRIESTHOOD OF ALL BELIEVERS

Priesthood of all believers is a term used by Martin Luther, who desired to reform the church. Because he thought that the bishops and priests in control were corrupt and incapable of reform, he appealed to the idea of the priesthood of all believers. This principle meant that carrying out church functions was not limited to ordained individuals. Thus Luther called upon the local rulers of Germany (for example, dukes and princes) to throw out the corrupt bishops and priests, and replace them with reform-minded ministers. These new ministers would have been educated at universities that taught the reform theology.

Anabaptists picked up on the idea that church leadership did not operate in a separate realm, inhabited only by priests. However, Anabaptists used this idea differently than Luther. Anabaptists applied this idea to the interpretation of scriptures. They believed that any community member, including women, could participate in reading and discussing the Bible. In other words, Anabaptists did not think that only ordained ministers could understand Biblical teachings.

Thus, sixteenth-century Anabaptist community members led their own Bible studies. They also selected leaders from among their group members rather than finding, or being given someone, from outside the group who held particular credentials. Anabaptists administered communion to one another rather than requiring a priest or minister to do so. Versions of these practices remain in place for Anabaptist congregations today.

A meeting of Swiss-origin Anabaptists in the open air under the triangular symbol for the eye of God. This drawing from the late 1500s shows what were probably church leaders discussing either the Bible or some church document. It was safer to have meetings and worship in more remote open-air settings.

Some North American Mennonites seek to understand their Anabaptist past and visit European scenes of origin. A remote cave in Canton Zurich, Switzerland, was used by Anabaptists centuries earlier as a secret place of gathering and worship. In 1987 a historical tour of Europe visited that cave. On the tour was elderly Lester Mann, who proved too weak for the steep climb. Wilmer Martin, Rolf Grude, and another tour member literally carried Mr. Mann up to the cave. These historical tours to this cave often include singing hymns, personal reflections, and sometimes even communion.

In the 1500s and 1600s the Hutterites of Moravia were sometimes called Habaner. They made beautiful ceramics, much prized then by the nobility and now by museums. Here is a reproduction of a Habaner plate.

Anabaptists in Moravia

NIKOLSBURG

Nikolsburg was a town in Moravia ruled by the Liechtenstein family. This family was known for being tolerant of Anabaptists. In fact, Leonhart von Liechtenstein even accepted adult baptism. Thus for a time Nikolsburg became a center of Anabaptist activity. Balthasar Hubmaier was its Anabaptist leader. Hubmaier had been an Anabaptist pastor in the town of Waldshut, near Zurich, but in Austrian territory. When the Austrians re-established Catholic control of Waldshut, Hubmaier fled to Nikolsburg. Many other Anabaptist refugees from Switzerland and the Tyrol also fled to Nikolsburg, looking for a place of relative safety. Among the Anabaptists in Nikolsburg were two distinct groups, the *Stäbler* and the *Schwertler*.

Stäbler

The *Stäbler* were a pacifist Anabaptist group living near Nikolsburg. *Stab* means staff in German. Those who made a point of not having a sword, but carrying only a staff, were called *Stäbler*. These Anabaptists were refugees from Switzerland and were following the witness of Conrad Grebel and Felix Mantz.

Schwertler

Schwert is the German word for sword. The *Schwertler* were a group of Nikolsburg Anabaptists who believed in using swords for defense. Balthasar Hubmaier was the leader of this group. Being well-established in the city, Hubmaier had the authority to forbid the *Stäbler* to meet within the city walls. Thus, the *Stäbler* met outside the city walls, under the leadership of Jacob Wiedemann and Philip Jäger.

BALTHASAR HVBMOR DOCTOR VON FRIDBERG.

Balthasar Hubmaier (1480?-1528) was a highly educated theologian in the Anabaptist movement in Moravia. At his trial in Vienna, he refused to recant (give up) his Anabaptist beliefs, so he was executed by burning at the stake in 1527. His wife Elizabeth was executed by drowning in the Danube River.

This drawing shows a Hutterite family in Moravia in the 1500s. The large house in the background suggests the communal approach to life that the Hutterites practiced, as they followed the description of the early church in Acts 4:32-37.

COMMUNITY OF GOODS
Community of goods is the practice of sharing and owning all things in common. In the practice of community of goods, the group owns all property together—no individual owns anything by her- or himself. The *Stäbler*, led by Jacob Wiedemann, eventually made it to the city of Austerlitz and established themselves as a community there. They continued to practice community of goods and developed theological reasons for continuing the practice, even after it was no longer necessary for survival. In 1540, Peter Riedemann wrote, "the Father [God] has nothing for himself, but everything he has, he has with the Son. Likewise, the Son has nothing for himself, but all he has, he has with the Father and all who have fellowship with him." This *Confession of Our Religion* became a definitive statement of faith for Hutterian Anabaptists.

In what ways does your congregation or community share resources?

Winter of 1528

In the winter of 1528, the *Stäbler* were officially expelled from the city of Nikolsburg. The group decided to make the long trek to Moravia, pooling their belongings together in order to survive. As the story is told, the exiles spread a blanket on the frozen ground on which to see what supplies they had; this was the start of the practice of community of goods.

JAKOB HUTTER

Jakob Hutter, a hat maker, first visited the Anabaptist colony at Austerlitz in 1529. He came from the Puster Valley in South Tyrol, a part of Austria. He was known for being strong and stubborn. Hutter joined as a member of the community, and soon became the community's representative in the Tyrol. Hutter introduced the practice of community of goods back in South Tyrol and also recruited people from there to immigrate to the Austerlitz community. As well, Hutter established connections for himself by visiting the Anabaptist communities in the neighboring towns of Auspitz and Rossitz.

Throughout this time, there were numerous conflicts between the Anabaptist leaders in this triangle of cities in Moravia. There were accusations of dishonesty among leaders; these accusations included holding secret funds of money, which would have been in direct violation of the practice of community of goods. Sometimes using authoritarian means and claiming divine inspiration, Hutter emerged by November 1533 as the dominant Anabaptist leader in Moravia. The Anabaptists in this area eventually became known as Hutterites, after Jakob Hutter. Hutterites today carry his name and continue the practice of community of goods.

In May 1535, the local political ruler, Lord Lippe, came under pressure from Archduke Ferdinand to expel all Anabaptists from his territories. Hutter confronted the authorities and wrote a strong letter of protest. His arrest was demanded, but Hutter temporarily avoided the authorities by returning to the Tyrol in July 1535.

Hutter continued his work as an Anabaptist organizer, and it was late November before he was finally arrested. In December Hutter was taken to Innsbruck, Archduke Ferdinand's seat of government. Hutter was tried, cruelly tortured, and burned at the stake in Innsbruck by mid-March 1536. Hutter remained stubbornly steadfast through this end-of-life ordeal.

FERDINAND, THE ARCHDUKE 1503-1564

In October 1526 Charles V (Emperor of the Holy Roman Empire) gave his brother Ferdinand control over family heritage lands in Moravia. Ferdinand launched major efforts to eradicate Anabaptists from that area. Persecution was especially harsh from 1534 -1537. Many Anabaptists fled from the region. Many others were executed, including leaders such as Balthasar Hubmaier, George Blaurock (who had previously escaped prison in Switzerland), and Jacob Hutter.

Ferdinand was the grandson of Queen Isabel of Castilla (Spain), who financed the travels of Christopher Columbus. It was also Queen Isabel and her husband Ferdinand (King of Aragon) who established the Inquisition in Spain in the previous century. The Inquisition was an attempt to expose heretics (non-believers). Suspects were forced to confess and repent, or face execution. The Spanish Inquisition was directed against converted Jews and Muslims who were suspected of secretly retaining their earlier beliefs. The result was intense persecution and eventually the expulsion of Jews from Spain. Later the Spanish Inquisition was expanded to include those suspected of being Protestants.

Austerlitz, Auspitz, and Rossitz

These three cities in Moravia attracted a large number of Anabaptists fleeing from persecuted areas in Germany and Switzerland. The cities formed a triangle, roughly twelve miles per side. The local ruler was relatively tolerant of Anabaptists, making this area a temporarily safe haven for refugees escaping danger in other places. (see map on page 8)

In 1526 Archduke Ferdinand I (1503-1564) was given control of Moravia by his brother, Charles V (Holy Roman Emperor). He began to persecute the Anabaptist Hutterites in his territories, especially from 1534 to 1537; leaders were executed and many fled.

This woodcut from a 1607 book was created by opponents of Hutterites. Using a tactic similar to political cartoons of today, the image criticizes the Hutterites by comparing them to doves living in a dovecoat house, who dirty their houses with their own refuse. A dovecoat is a birdhouse built for communally living birds.

Ausbund hymnal, first published in 1564 in Europe. This is a 1785 edition published in Germantown (now Philadelphia).

PHILIPPITES

Among the Anabaptists in Moravia, the Philippites were followers of Philipp Plener. The group had originally arrived in Moravia in 1529 but soon moved to Auspitz to establish their community. Like the other Anabaptist groups in Moravia, the Philippites organized around the practice of community of goods. Eventually the harsh measures of Archduke Ferdinand caused the Philippites to flee the region.

The group left Moravia, traveling in small groups toward the Palatinate and southern Germany. One group of about fifty travelers and three leaders was arrested and imprisoned in 1535 in the dungeon of the fortress at Passau. While in prison, members of this group wrote a number of hymns that were saved and later edited into a collection of 53 hymns published in 1564. These hymns were later included in the *Ausbund*, the hymnal still used by Amish congregations today.

The fate of all those imprisoned in Passau is not known. Some were tortured but not killed. Some recanted and were released. Others died in prison. Some eventually joined the Swiss Anabaptists. This joining led to an early misperception that the hymns from Passau were written by Swiss Anabaptists.

How does knowing the story of the Philippites affect how you hear or sing the hymn: *The word of God is solid ground?*

THE WORD OF GOD IS SOLID GROUND

The word of God is solid ground,
our constant firm confession,
No source of freedom more profound,
no purer a profession.
All steadfast strength, all breadth and length
of truth, from God's word springing
Shall we employ to speak our joy,
this world our witness bringing.

What powers can our faith constrain?
What iron-clad restrictions?
No self-deceiving rule can chain
our conscience and convictions.
Our God alone is on the throne,
and we are subjects willing.
Our lives obey God's higher way;
our love God's law fulfilling.

What God-word brings, may we embrace;
success and suffering greet us;
confronting evil face to face,
as scorn and anger meet us.
For freedom's sake we bend, we break,
a sign to every nation
that we have found a solid ground;
God's word our sure foundation.

Today some Mennonites and Brethren still get inspiration from the earliest generation of Anabaptists. This hymn text from the 1992 *Hymnal: A Worship Book*, here translated as "The word of God is solid ground," was written by an anonymous Anabaptist of the Hutterite persuasion imprisoned in Passau. It was printed in the 1564 *Ausbund* hymnal, probably the oldest currently- and continuously-used hymnal among Christian groups in North America. Old Order Amish still use this hymnal.

35

These replica cages hang high on the exterior of St. Lambert Church in the German city of Münster. They are reminders of the actual cages in which the bodies of Jan van Leiden, Bernhard Knipperdolling, and Bernhard Krechting were left to rot after the Münsterite revolt was thwarted.

The City of Münster

MELCHIOR HOFFMAN (ca. 1495-1543)

Melchior Hoffman was born in Schwäbisch Hall, in southern Germany. He was a furrier by trade. In 1523 he took a position as a Lutheran minister at a church in Lavonia. Hoffman's theology often focused on the endtimes.

The term *endtimes* refers to the time and events thought to accompany the return of Jesus to earth. Endtimes theology fits within the larger discussion of eschatology; eschatology is how one understands the culmination of the reign of Jesus on earth. There are many sixteenth-century and modern-day understandings of what this might mean. Some expect that the end will involve a huge battle in which Jesus is physically present and the godless are destroyed; others suggest that the reign of Jesus is an ever-present invitation to live within the kingdom of God in daily life on earth.

Hoffman's endtimes theology came from his understanding of the book of Revelation. Hoffman thought he was the endtimes witness mentioned in Revelation 11:3 and that major changes on earth would occur in 1533. This radical theology got him expelled from Lavonia.

After some moves, Hoffman went to the city of Dorpat and served as reform pastor there. A story told from this time period is that one day the daughter of the Dorpat mayor appeared in church wearing a necklace made from melted communion vessels. The vessels had been confiscated from the church as part of Hoffman's reform. Hoffman was outraged at their new form. He sarcastically asked the congregation members to kneel down and worship the sacred ornaments carried in procession into the sanctuary. Inflammatory actions such as this, as well as his eschatological preaching, eventually got Hoffman expelled from Dorpat.

Starting in January 1529, Hoffman traveled for five months with Andreas Karlstadt, a reform leader and colleague of Martin Luther. Hoffman and Karlstadt went to Schlieswieg-Holstein and East Friesland. Though Karlstadt

Melchior Hoffman (1495-1543) spread Anabaptism in his many travels, especially to the Netherlands and northern Germany. He spent time in prison in Strasbourg.

Jan Matthijs from the Netherlands became the initial leader of the Münsterite Anabaptists. He believed that violence could be used to bring about the kingdom of God on earth. In 1534 he was killed in a battle against forces of the authorities who had put Münster under siege. The peaceful wing of Anabaptism spent centuries convincing people not to associate all Anabaptists with the violent Anabaptists of Münster.

was not an Anabaptist himself, discussions that the pair had about baptism probably paved the way for Hoffman's decision to join the Anabaptist movement, which was soon to come.

Following his travels with Karlstadt, Hoffman went to Strasbourg, where he was initially welcomed by reform pastor Martin Bucer. Hoffman's acceptance of Anabaptism occurred sometime while in Strasbourg. Eventually Hoffman faced arrest in Strasbourg when he petitioned for a public space for Anabaptists to worship.

Hoffman then traveled north into the Low Countries, continuing to preach. He baptized approximately three hundred people in Emden, Netherlands, in June 1530. This is considered the introduction of Anabaptism in the Low Countries. Hoffman continued traveling throughout this region from 1530-34, baptizing followers. His primary concern was not that of establishing congregations, but of preparing people for the endtimes that he thought was coming. The followers of Hoffman were called Melchiorites.

When ten of Hoffman's followers (including Bible study leader Sikke Freerks Snijder) were executed in the Hague in December 1531, Hoffman was shocked into calling a *Stillstand*—a halt of adult baptisms for two years. Jan Matthijs, who had earlier been baptized by Hoffman, dismissed the call for a *Stillstand* and seized leadership of a faction of Hoffman's followers.

In 1533 Hoffman was imprisoned in Strasbourg. He died in prison ten years later.

JAN MATTHIJS (JAN, SON OF MATTHEW)

Jan Matthijs, a baker by trade, was from the city of Haarlem in the Low Countries. Shrugging off the reluctance of Hoffman to continue with baptisms, Jan Matthijs actively sought followers from among the Melchiorites.

Jan Matthijs moved to the city of Münster in January 1534. There, Jan Matthijs persuaded Bernhard Rothmann, the lead pastor of the Münster church, that the time had come to make a sharp break with the established church. Jan Matthijs declared the city of Münster under his control and called for the deaths of all those who refused adult baptism. However, Bernhard Knipperdolling (who would later become mayor of Münster under the leadership of Matthijs) exercised a moderating influence.

Knipperdolling persuaded Jan Matthijs to give citizens one week to leave the city unharmed if they did not accept baptism and the new leadership. Bishop Franz Waldeck, who had withdrawn from Münster, established a military siege outside the city boundaries.

Jan Matthijs declared Münster a city of refuge and his representatives invited people from across the region to come there; he believed the city would be ready to receive Jesus, whom Jan Matthijs declared would return at Easter 1534 to wipe out the wicked. Rothmann became the movement's theological spokesperson, authoring the book *Van der Wreke,* which defended their use of the sword against the godless. In the city Jan Matthijs ruled with absolute authority; he killed, or threatened to kill, any dissidents.

Jan Matthijs established the practice of community of goods in Münster. Though Rothmann wrote a piece defending the theology of community of goods, the practice may have been instituted more out of necessity than ideology, due to the fact that no supplies were moving in or out of the city because of Bishop Waldeck's siege.

When the predicted miraculous events did not occur at Easter 1534, Jan Matthijs decided to take matters into his own hands. On April 4, 1534, he led a military attack against the forces of Bishop Waldeck. Jan Matthijs was killed in this battle.

It is possible that Jan van Leiden (a follower of Jan Matthijs) provoked Jan Matthijs into attempting such a military move, hoping to create an opportunity in which leadership would change hands. And it happened; Jan van Leiden became the new leader of the Anabaptists in Münster.

JAN VAN LEIDEN — "KING JAN"

Jan van Leiden came from the city of Leiden in the Netherlands. He had worked as a tailor, a merchant, and an innkeeper; he also liked to act in the theater; King David was his favorite role to play. Jan van Leiden was baptized on November 1, 1533, by Jan Matthijs.

King Jan (as he now called himself) set up a throne in the downtown marketplace of Münster. There he held court, wearing royal symbols on a chain around his neck. King Jan also instituted polygamy and took several wives himself. When one of his wives challenged his authority, he had her executed in the public square and then trod on her body. Others who spoke against him faced similar fates.

As the siege by Bishop Waldeck and his army tightened, conditions inside the city worsened. King Jan sent the women and children out of Münster. Many of these women and children were captured and killed. Eventually a guard betrayed the city by telling Bishop Waldeck's forces where they could enter the city. On June 25, 1535, the bishop attacked the city with 3000 men. Most of the 800 men defending the city were killed over the next two days.

JOHAN BEVCKELS VON CLEYDEN.

Jan van Leiden became the new leader of the Münsterite Anabaptists in 1534. He declared himself a king, instituted polygamy, and executed his opponents. A siege by the more powerful Catholic forces ended in the slaughter of hundreds, including the three leaders.

How would you view the Anabaptist movement if these sixteenth-century Münsterites were the only Anabaptists you knew?

S. MARGARETA.

Jan van Leiden, mayor Bernhard Knipperdolling, and council member Bernhard Kretching were captured alive. After being put on display for several weeks, the three men were tortured and then killed by having their hearts pierced with a hot dagger. Their bodies were put in cages and hung on the tower of St. Lambert's church in the city square. Replicas of the cages remain in view today.

RESPONSE TO MÜNSTER

Jan Matthijs had established the Anabaptist kingdom in Münster with the expectation that Jesus would return there. Jan Matthijs had taken Hoffman's view of the endtimes but shifted the origin of the revolution from above to below. In other words, while Hoffman had left the endtimes process in the hands of God, the Münsterites thought that their violent actions would bring about the return of Jesus.

In August 1536 Anabaptist leaders gathered in Bocholt. The meeting was to discuss the future of the Dutch Anabaptist movement, in light of the recent catastrophic events in Münster. David Joris was present at this meeting and suggested a compromise between those who advocated continued violent revolution and those who pushed for a nonviolent direction. David's proposal was that the idea of vengeance towards the godless could be kept but that people could rely on God to carry out the punishment. Thus, though the thought was still violent, the application of the belief did not require violent actions from people. At this time, David Joris was the most prominent of the non-Münsterite Anabaptists.

Emerging Anabaptist leader Menno Simons offered a different understanding of the endtimes, which gradually came to wide acceptance. Menno believed not in a specific endtimes location (such as Münster) but suggested that people develop a consciousness of living in a time of grace that had begun with Jesus. Menno believed that the church was called to be a new Jerusalem in the midst of the wicked world. In other words, he thought that followers of Jesus were to live out the peaceful reign of God wherever they happened to be, until the time that Jesus would return. The followers of Menno have carried this legacy of a visible nonviolent kingdom into the present day.

How can you live out the peaceful reign of God in your community?

A drawing (1606) depicting the execution of leaders of the Münsterite rebellion on a platform near St. Lambert Church. Note the three iron cages attached to the church.

"Christ has not taken His kingdom with the sword, but He entered it through much suffering. Oh, blindness of man!"

"All of you who would fight with the sword of David and also be servants of the Lord, consider these words. If he is not to strive and quarrel, how then can he fight? If he is to be gentle to all men, how can he then hate and harm them?. . . If he is to instruct in meekness those that oppose, how can he destroy them?"

—*Menno Simons,*
"The Blasphemy of John of Leiden"

For no one can lay any foundation other than the one already laid, which is Jesus Christ.

1 Cor. 3:11

Why was 1 Corinthians 3:11 significant to Menno?

Menno Simons

MENNO AS PRIEST

Menno Simons is the individual after whom Mennonites are named. He was born about 1496 in Witmarsum, Friesland, in the Netherlands. He was trained as a priest. His first parish was in Pingjum where he served from 1524-1531. While a priest, Menno came to question the established church teaching on communion. By turning to the scriptures, he came to believe that the communion bread and wine did not actually turn into the body and blood of Jesus.

Menno also began to examine what the church was saying about baptism. Again, Menno turned to scripture reading, and he reached the conclusion that baptizing infants was an errant practice. He could find no mention of infant baptism in the scriptures but instead found the call to believers (meaning adults, of accountable age) to join with Jesus.

The execution of Anabaptist Sikke Freerks Snyder (the first execution in the Low Countries) likely influenced Menno's sense of immediacy and spurred him into study of baptism. He was horrified that the church would execute a man, and he was also amazed that a person would hold a faith so strongly that he would remain steadfast even unto death.

Shortly thereafter, however, Menno was promoted to be a priest in his hometown of Witmarsum. He accepted the position, even though by this time he had started to have real doubts about the religious life he was living, including the rejection of two significant sacraments of the church: the Lord's Supper and infant baptism.

Created in 1948 by a Dutch Mennonite, this striking image of Menno Simons emphasizes his devotion to using the Scriptures as the standard for Christian faith. Although Menno had to flee from various locations, he found refuge in northern Germany and died there of natural causes.

This engraving by Christoffel van Sichem was created about 45 years after Menno's death. One of the earliest portraits of Menno, the artist took care to include Menno's Bible and crutch. Menno wrote extensively and taught Anabaptist congregations in the Netherlands, and what is now Germany and Poland, as far as Danzig.

REACTION TO MÜNSTER

While still a priest, Menno had conversations with emissaries from the revolutionary Anabaptist kingdom of Münster. Menno found their violence and "false faith" troubling. Menno was also likely disturbed by the bloody events at the Oldeklooster. The Oldeklooster was a monastery near Bolsward in Friesland that had been overthrown by revolutionary Anabaptists associated with Münster. When the forces of Emperor Charles V retook control of the monastery, lives were lost. One of those killed was Peter Simons, who may have been a brother to Menno. It was at this point that Menno wrote *The Blasphemy of John of Leiden.* This short tract likely circulated in manuscript form but was not published until 1627.

In his tract, Menno described the Münsterites in this way:
> "Christ has not taken His kingdom with the sword, but He entered it through much suffering. Yet they think to take it by the sword! Oh, blindness of man! But thus it must be, that those who will not confess Christ their only Shepherd so that they may be pastured by Him, will have to eat of the pastures which are trampled upon; and that those who will not draw the clear crystal water from the fount of the Saviour, will have to drink the impure water which the false shepherds have stirred up with their feet. . . .They have forsaken the Lord, the living fountain, and have made fountains of their own which appear beautiful but they afford no water. . . . Let every one of you guard against all strange doctrine of swords and resistance and other like things which is nothing short of a fair flower under which lies hidden an evil serpent which has shot his venom into many. Let every one beware." (p. 49 of *Complete Writings*)

JOINING THE ANABAPTISTS

While still a young priest, Menno got to know brothers Dirk and Obbe Phillips. Dirk and Obbe were leaders of the Anabaptist movement in Leeuwarden, Netherlands. These Anabaptists followed the teachings of Melchior Hoffman. When Menno finally left the priesthood in January 1536, he sought out these peaceful Anabaptists. Menno was likely baptized and ordained by Obbe Philips. Menno was soon recognized as a leader in Obbe's faction of Melchiorite Anabaptists.

Menno traveled widely across the Netherlands, North Germany, as far as today's Poland, and into the Danzig and Vistula Delta region. In these travels he preached and taught in Anabaptist communities scattered throughout this area. The name *Mennonite* was first used to describe the Anabaptists in areas where Menno ministered.

ESCAPE FROM AUTHORITIES

Throughout his life, Menno was pursued by authorities who arrested Anabaptists. One story is told about Menno riding on top of a stagecoach, sitting by the driver. Officials searching for Menno stopped the carriage and asked if Menno was inside. Menno leaned over, pulled open the carriage door, and asked, "Is Menno Simons inside?" When the people inside answered no, Menno calmly told the Anabaptist hunters that Menno was not inside. The officials went on their way, still searching for Menno. Though the story is likely apocryphal (meaning legendary, or mythical), it nonetheless illustrates Menno's uncanny ability to stay ahead of the law.

FAMILY LIFE

When and where Menno married Gertrud is not known. It is thought that they had at least three children. Gertrud shared the hardships of her husband's life as a hunted Anabaptist preacher.

The last seven years of Menno's life were spent in the village of Wüstenfelde. Wüstenfelde belonged to the estate of the nobleman Bartholomew von Ahlefeldt, who granted exile to Mennonite refugees fleeing persecution.

Menno died on January 31, 1561, of natural causes.

WRITINGS OF MENNO

All of Menno's tracts and books had I Corinthians 3:11 printed on the title page:

"For no one can lay any foundation other than the one that has been laid; that foundation is Jesus Christ."

This verse establishes Menno's theology, which is to use the life of Jesus as a guide.

Menno writes:

". . . then contrast your desire with Christ's, your doctrine with Christ's, your spirit with Christ's, and your life with Christ's. Then you will discover whether you are in or out of Christ, who is your God, what Lord you serve, and of

In Pingjum, the Netherlands, a so-called "secret" church, is a Mennonite meetinghouse, which from the outside looks like a dwelling. Menno Simons served as a Roman Catholic priest in Pingjum from 1524 to 1531, after which he renounced his Roman Catholicism and joined the Anabaptist movement. This particular home of the Mennonite congregation was from a much later time.

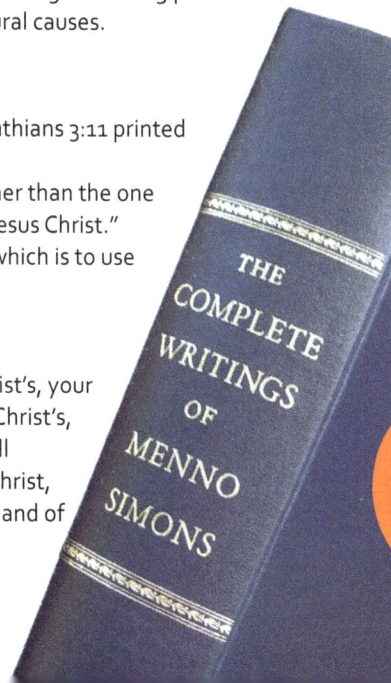

This 1956 English translation (ca. 1,000 pages) of all known writings by Menno illustrates continued North American interest in his life and thought.

What do you think Menno would write about if he were alive today?

(Adapted from several of Menno's texts, by Kenneth Nafziger. Found in *Sing the Story*, #61.)

O God, to whom then shall I turn?
Come, now protect me as I wander. I
am surrounded day and night by foes
that seek my soul to slander. O God,
your spirit grant to me so I in life might
faithful be, and in your presence dwell
eternally.

Wand'ring alone through Egypt's land,
daily I sinned, your Name renouncing.
There I was seen a worthy guest,
untroubled by the world around me.
Trapped, without hope, in evil's noose,
not fearing I my life might lose, I gave
myself unto the devil's cause.

But I returned to God, my Lord, once
and for all the world forsaking. Riches
of Egypt faded soon as Christ his peace
eternal gave me. They who desire to
enter life, though in a world where sin is
rife, must stay the course through trials,
tests and strife.

Then at the end of life's short span,
Christ, our salvation, there awaits us.
"Come child," says God, "receive your
crown; here dwell forever with the
angels." Tears shall be wiped from ev'ry
eye. No one will suffer pain or die. Let us
Christ Jesus' name now glorify!

Menno's stages of life are revealed in the different stanzas. Verse one describes his current reality of life as a fugitive due to his Anabaptist faith; verse two recalls his life as a priest; verse three talks of his conversion; verse four looks to peace and salvation through Jesus Christ.

what kind of spirit and kingdom you are the children." (p. 209, *Complete Writings*)

Menno was a staunch pacifist, which was evident in many of his texts. In 1552, he wrote:

"The prince of peace is Jesus Christ. . . . True Christians do not know vengeance. . . . They are the children of peace. . . . they walk in the way of peace."

In a frequently quoted text from 1539, Menno writes:

"True evangelical faith is of such a nature that it cannot lie dormant; it clothes the naked; it feeds the hungry; it comforts the sorrowful; it shelters the destitute; it aids and consoles the sad; it returns good for evil; it serves those that harm it; it prays for those that persecute it; it teaches, admonishes, and reproves with the Word of the Lord; it seeks that which is lost; it binds up that which is wounded; it heals that which is diseased and it saves that which is sound; it has become all things to all men."

THE FOUNDATION BOOK
(The Foundation of Christian Doctrine)

Menno's *Foundation Book (Dat Fundament des Christelycken leers)* was first published in 1539-40. This was Menno's comprehensive faith statement. He revised and published it again in 1554 and was working on a third edition at the time of his death.

In the *Foundation Book*, Menno describes his Anabaptist beliefs. Of baptism he writes:

"Christ, after His resurrection, commanded His apostles saying, Go ye therefore, and teach all nations, baptizing them in the name of the Father, and of the Son, and the Holy Ghost; teaching them to observe all things whatsoever I have commanded

Are Menno's writings still relevant?

you; . . . Here we have the Lord's commandment concerning baptism, as to when according to the ordinance of God it shall be administered and received; namely, that the Gospel must first be preached, and then those baptized who believe it. . . . Faith does not follow from baptism, but baptism follows from faith." (page 120, from *Complete Writings*)

His writings reveal his intent to make a clear separation of the Anabaptist movement from the use of violence. Menno writes:

"Christ is our fortress; patience our weapon of defense; the Word of God our sword; and our victory a courageous, firm, unfeigned faith in Jesus Christ. And iron and metal spears and swords we leave to those who, alas, regard human blood and swine's blood about alike. He that is wise let him judge what I mean." (page 198 of *Complete Writings*)

Of faith and grace Menno writes:

"The Gospel is the blessed announcement of the favor and grace of God to us, and of forgiveness of sins through Jesus Christ." (page 115 of *Complete Writings*)

He contrasts this understanding with the established church practice that said that the taking of communion (bread and wine consecrated by a priest) was what was necessary to receive forgiveness of sin. Menno writes:

"But those who name themselves by the name of the Lord, worship, honor, and serve a piece of bread and a mouthful of wine as the actual flesh and blood of Christ. . . . Oh, unbearable abomination and shame that the praise of God, the glory of Jesus Christ, should be converted and changed into such an impotent idol which can neither execute vengeance, or speak, hear, see, stand on its feet, or walk away, which worms eat and time consumes, which has to be locked up, preserved, helped, and carried about by the hands of men just like the idols of Babylon as Baruch relates." (page 154 of *Complete Writings*)

Menno signed his writing, "By me, M.S."

CONNECTION TO SWISS ANABAPTISTS

Swiss Anabaptist refugees learned of Menno's writings in the 1600s when Dutch Mennonites reached out to them, offering material aid and assistance in immigrating to North America. Swiss Anabaptists picked up the name *Mennonites* by their association with these Dutch Mennonites. When they arrived in North America, they were called Mennonites and have carried that name since.

EINEN ANDERN GRUND KANN NIEMAND LEGEN AUSER DEM DER GELEGT IST WELCHER IST JESUS CHRISTUS 1KOR3 11

This German motto, locally carved, hangs on the wall of the sanctuary at Winkler Bergthaler Mennonite Church, Winkler, Manitoba. The same verse (1 Corinthians 3:11) appears in English on the exterior of the church building (see page 42).

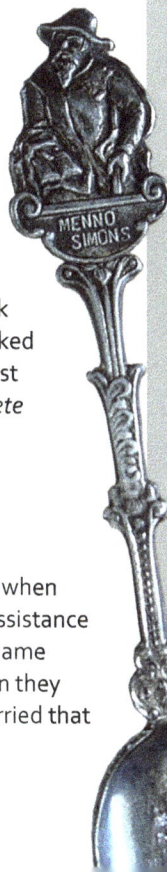

In 1961 the Dutch Mennonites produced a commemorative small spoon with an image of Menno Simons on the handle top, marking the 400th anniversary of his death. In 1996 the Dutch Mennonites commemorated the 500th anniversary of the birth of Menno with this sandwich box.

47

Het Bloedig Tooneel,

OF

MARTELAERS

SPIEGEL

DER

DOOPS-GESINDE

OF

Weereloose Christenen,

Die/ om 't getuygenis van JESUS haren Salighmaker/ geleden hebben
ende gedood zijn/ van CHRISTI tijd af/ tot desen tijd toe.

Versamelt uyt verscheyde geloofweerdige Chronijken, Memorien, en Getuygenissen.

Door T. J. V. BRAGHT.

Den Tweeden Druk.

Bysonder vermeerdert met vele Autentijke Stucken, en over de hond... curieuse Konstplaten.

FAC ET SPERA.

T'AMSTERDAM,

By J. vander DEYSTER, H. vanden BERG, JAN BLOM, Wed. S. SWART, ...
S. WYBRANDS, en A. OSSAAN. En Compagnie. 1685.
Met Privilegie.

The *Martyrs Mirror* has stories of Christian martyrs beginning with Jesus and ending with those from the 1600s. It has shaped an Anabaptist understanding of faith for more than 350 years. The title page of the 1685 second edition, in the Dutch language, has an image of a spading man with the Latin words, "*Fac et Spera*," which means "Do/Work and Hope." It points to farming and the hope that faith brings to the believer. The leather and metal straps enabled the covers to hang together.

Martyrs Mirror

MARTYR

The word *martyr* means to witness. To be martyred means to witness to one's faith, by and through death. A martyr's death was a testimony that what the martyr believed was of higher value than whatever it was that the torturers were trying to make the martyr say or do. The Anabaptists saw martyrdom as a public witness of faithfulness. In the territories of Switzerland, Moravia, Austria, Germany, and the Netherlands, several thousand Anabaptists were martyred during the sixteenth century.

Some Anabaptists sang hymns as they were being put to death. Government and church officials feared this powerful witness and sometimes cut out the tongues of those who were to be executed so that they could not speak or sing in the moments before death. Sometimes tongue screws were used.

MARTYRS MIRROR

The *Martyrs Mirror* is a collection of stories of sixteenth-century Anabaptist martyrs; included also are stories of martyrs from the early church. It was compiled by Thieleman J. van Braght in 1660 and published first in Dutch in the Netherlands. The first English edition of *Martyrs Mirror* appeared in 1837. It has been reprinted in five English editions since then. The North American Mennonite publishing house, now called MennoMedia, has published *Martyrs Mirror* since 1938, continuing until the present day. In translation, the book's full title is *The Bloody Theater or Martyrs Mirror of the Defenseless Christians Who Baptized Only Upon Confession of Faith, and Who Suffered and Died for the Testimony of Jesus, Their Savior, From the Time of Christ to the Year A.D. 1660.* This long title follows the earlier practice of attempting to summarize the book in the title.

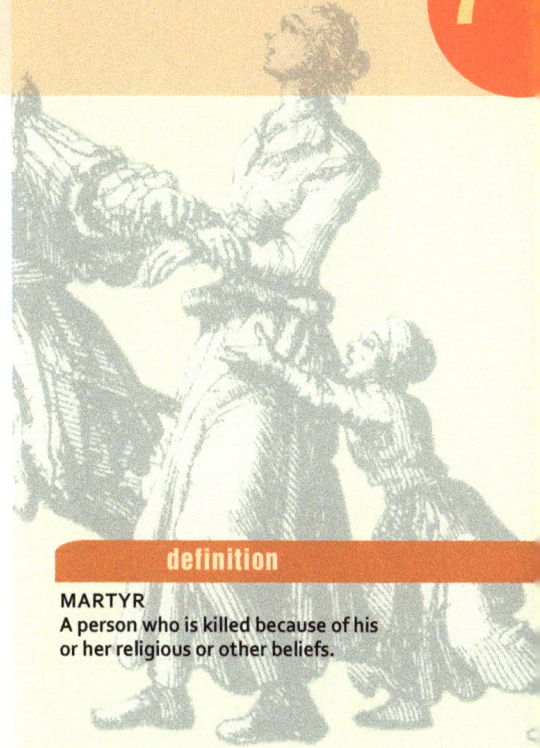

definition

MARTYR
A person who is killed because of his or her religious or other beliefs.

Aus tiefer Noth schrei' ich zu dir

O Lord God, You are our shield;
toward You we turn.
For us it is a minor pain
when they take our lives.
You have prepared eternity for us.
So when we suffer
shame and stress here,
it is not for nothing.

(Ausbund No. 61, p. 329-331, stanza 6: Tune
NUN FREUT EUCH, 1523-24)

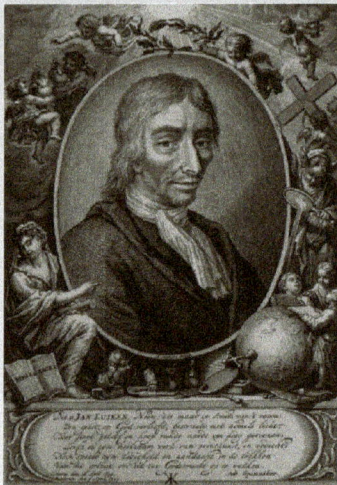

Jan Luyken (1649-1712) was an accomplished Dutch Mennonite engraver and poet who created copper plates used to illustrate the 1685 *Martyrs Mirror*.

Edited by Kirsten Beachy, this collection of poems, stories, and essays (Herald Press, 2010) reflects the varied reactions of contemporary readers of *Martyrs Mirror* (used with permission).

THIELEMAN VAN BRAGHT

Thieleman Van Braght was a cloth merchant and also a conservative, theologically-learned elder in the Flemish Mennonite Church of Dordrecht. Van Braght was concerned about divisions among Dutch Mennonites. In producing *Martyrs Mirror,* he intentionally used stories from two opposing Dutch Mennonite leaders, Hans de Ries and Pieter Jansz Twisck. Each of these men had published an edition of a martyrs book that emphasized the tradition from which he came: de Ries represented the liberal Waterlanders and Twisck spoke for the conservative Dutch Mennonites. Van Braght's compilation, then, was an effort to show that both viewpoints could find unity in the living witness of the martyrs.

JAN LUYKEN

The second edition of *Martyrs Mirror* (published in 1685) contained 104 illustrations by the artist Jan Luyken. These illustrations were prints from copper plates. Van Braght died before this second edition was printed.

Thirty-one of Jan Luyken's 104 original copper plates are known to have survived. Seven were acquired by Old Order Mennonite historian Amos Hoover in 1977. In 1988, twenty-three additional plates became available and were purchased by the Martyrs Mirror Trust, organized by John Oyer and Robert Kreider. In 1990 these plates were developed by Oyer and Kreider into a traveling exhibit called "Mirror of the Martyrs." The display is now housed at Kauffman Museum in North Newton, Kansas. One additional plate, an engraving showing Anabaptist martyr Jacques d'Auchy bidding farewell to his grieving wife, surfaced in 2011 and was likewise acquired by the Martyrs Mirror Trust.

STORIES OF THE MARTYRS

Dirk Willems (d. 1569)

Dirk Willems was an Anabaptist living in the city of Asperen, Netherlands. Like many other Anabaptists at that time, his life was in danger due to his faith practices. Dirk was imprisoned but managed to flee his captors. He escaped his pursuers by successfully crossing a frozen river. However, the man following him broke through a patch of thin ice, and was on the point of drowning. Dirk

returned to the spot, and pulled his pursuer out of the water. Though the man he saved may have been willing to let Dirk go as thanks for Dirk's help, the magistrate following them forced the man to arrest Dirk. Dirk was burned at the stake outside the town of Asperen on May 16, 1569.

A well-known print in *Martyrs Mirror* depicts Dirk Willems reaching back to pull his pursuer to safety.

Maeyken Wens (d. 1573)

Maeyken Wens was an Anabaptist martyr. She was burned at the stake in Antwerp, Belgium, on October 6, 1573. There is a print in *Martyrs Mirror* showing Maeyken's fifteen-year old son, Adriaen, searching the ashes after his mother was burned. His younger brother stands beside him, watching. Adriaen was looking for the tongue screw that the executioners used to keep his mother from speaking and witnessing to onlookers as she faced death. Before her death, Maeyken wrote letters from her prison cell to her Anabaptist husband and to Adriaen. The letters tell that she was frightened of death but hopeful of a richer life after death. Maeyken instructed Adriaen to take care of his younger brother.

Are there reasons to tell, or not to tell, these martyr stories?

Maeyken Wens was burned at the stake in 1573. A library in Amsterdam has an original letter written by Maeyken, perhaps the only such original letter of any Anabaptist martyr noted in *Martyrs Mirror*.

URSULA AND MARIA VON BECKUM
Ursula and Maria von Beckum were executed in 1544. The Amish hymnal, the *Ausbund*, contains a hymn which remembers their story.

Ausbund No 17, stanza 8:
Ursula, wife of a noble, in danger and distress, lovingly gives up her own body to bitter death. Love is stronger than any other force on earth. Hell, death, every other power, must fade away. Love comes from God.

Are there places in the world today where people are martyred for their faith?

The "Mirror of the Martyrs" exhibit at the Kauffman Museum in North Newton, Kansas.

The Drummer of Leeuwarden

There was a certain drummer living in the town of Leeuwarden. As drummer, he was officially part of the town's military company. However, not having to go marching or mount guard on a regular basis, he spent most of his days working in a shop in town. At his workplace was a pious, Anabaptist man named Sikke Snijder. The drummer held the greatest of respect for Sikke. Therefore, when Sikke was arrested for the crime of being Anabaptist and a date set for his execution, the drummer was horrified. What made it all the worse was that, as a member of the company, he was expected to be present at the execution, forming a circle around the condemned man so that no one from the crowd might try to free him.

The drummer asked his wife, Hadewijk, what she thought he ought to do. Hadewijk advised him to go as ordered. So, in order to dull the pain he knew he would feel, the drummer decided to get himself intoxicated for the event. But, rather than dulling his senses the alcohol loosened his tongue. Instead of standing quietly, the drummer began to preach loudly to the crowd of Sikke's piety and virtue. And he did not stop there. The drummer went on to name the authorities and clergy as the wicked ones in this event. Some of the spectators laughed. Others took the drummer's words to heart. Still others said, "He is crazy," and, "The drummer is drunk."

When the drummer sobered up, he realized the depth of his trouble. He had publicly defended an Anabaptist and called into question the actions of the state and church authorities. The drummer therefore decided to leave his company post, the city of Leeuwarden, and the state church in order to join the Anabaptists.

FRANCONIA CONFERENCE IN PENNSYLVANIA

In 1745, Mennonites in the Franconia Conference of Pennsylvania wrote to Mennonites in Amsterdam, asking for assistance to publish a German translation of the *Martyrs Mirror*. This occurred after the declaration of "King George's War." This war was the colonial component of a much larger war in Europe between England on one side and France and Spain on the other. The colonial component occurred primarily on Cape Breton Island in Nova Scotia. The proximity of this fighting, along with years of previous rumors, clearly concerned the pacifist Mennonites. The Franconia Mennonites feared that their young people were insufficiently schooled in their nonresistant faith, and they believed that reading the stories of early Anabaptist martyrs would be instructive.

When help from Amsterdam was not forthcoming, the Franconia Mennonites turned for help to the Seventh Day Brethren living at Ephrata. A member of the Brethren did the translation of *Martyrs Mirror* from Dutch into German, and their print shop published the giant book of some 1400 large pages. It was the largest book printed in America before the Revolutionary War of 1776. The title page gives 1748 as the date of publication, but due to production difficulties it was likely a couple years before complete copies were available.

This image from 1685 *Martyrs Mirror* shows Anabaptist Dirk Willems rescuing his pursuer. Without a doubt the most widely-known image from *Martyrs Mirror*, one librarian has collected more than 250 artistic recreations.

Esther Augsburger, Mennonite artist, and her son Michael created this large metal sculpture ("Guns to Plowshares") in 1997. They used partially-melted handguns to depict a plowshare—a peaceful tool for planting. Christians and Jews look to Isaiah 2:4 where the author envisions a time of peace when "they shall beat their swords into plowshares, and their spears into pruning hooks. Nation shall not lift up sword against nation, neither shall they learn war anymore." The sculpture, a sermon in metal, stands in a public setting in Washington, D. C.

Women of the Anabaptist Movement

Women were a part of the Anabaptist movement. The understanding of the priesthood of all believers applied to women as well as men. Women witnessed through martyrdom, opened their homes to Anabaptist gatherings, and participated in Bible reading and discussions. Women occasionally took on congregational leadership positions or shared life experiences as spouse to an Anabaptist preacher. Women were among the Anabaptist hymn-writers.

A handful of profiles are shared here; stories like these, however, are likely repeated for many unnamed women of the sixteenth century.

ANNEKEN JANS (d. 1571)

Anneken Jans was an Anabaptist who was martyred for her beliefs. A follower of the Anabaptist leader David Joris, Anneken was arrested in Rotterdam, Netherlands. She was drowned there on January 24, 1539. In *Martyrs Mirror* she is called Anna of Rotterdam.

As Anneken walked to the place where she was to be killed, she clutched her six-year-old son Isaiah in her arms. She held up a bag of money and offered it to anyone who would care for Isaiah. A baker took Isaiah, in spite of his wife's protest that their six children were already enough.

Anneken left a letter for her son Isaiah, advising him to follow Jesus in the little flock of Anabaptists. Isaiah grew up in the baker's family. He never accepted his mother's faith. Isaiah prospered for a time as a brewer and served as mayor of Rotterdam from 1580-81 and again from 1589-90. However, after a change in fortune, he died in poverty around the year 1602.

Women in Swiss dress from the 1531 Froschauer Bible.

HELENA VON FREYBERG (ca. 1491-1545)

Helena von Freyberg was born about 1491 and grew up in a noble family in Reith, near the town of Kitzbuehel. Her parents and Pilgram Marpeck's parents knew each other. Helena's husband, Onophrius von Freyberg, came from the nobility. Her husband remained a Lutheran throughout his life.

Helena was baptized in 1527 and turned her castle in Reith into a center of Anabaptist activity. She became the leader of a congregation that met there. Pilgram Marpeck may have visited this community.

In 1529, an order for Helena's arrest was issued. This occurred following a visit by Helena to a group of imprisoned Anabaptists. Helena fled the area. Archduke Ferdinand ordered the confiscation of her property. However, her sons intervened and they retained ownership.

In 1530 Helena moved to Constance. Here she continued to engage in Anabaptist activities. She hosted gatherings in her home. City officials warned her about sheltering Anabaptists. Her friendship with Marpeck, who was resisting officials in Strasbourg, further worried the Constance officials. Thus, in 1532, Helena's property was once again confiscated and she was expelled from Constance.

After a short time in Augsburg, Helena returned to the Tyrol. Discussions began with the government in Innsbruck about a recantation. A recantation was a statement that said that the sinner (in this case, Helena) was confessing her wrongdoings and promising to turn from her errant path. Civil authorities pushed for a public recantation but Helena held out for a private one. Eventually Helena won this argument. In October 1534 she made a private recantation, promising to turn away from Anabaptism.

However, to avoid almost certainly being arrested again, Helena left Tyrol. As far as is known, she never returned. She moved to Augsburg and hosted Anabaptist meetings in her home there. Helena was an intermediary between Marpeck and Caspar Schwenckfeld, carrying letters between them. Helena participated in the Marpeck circle, a network of Anabaptist congregations associated with Austerlitz.

Helena was expelled from Augsburg for a time, due to her Anabaptist activity. However, her two surviving sons wrote to officials in Augsburg and asked that their widowed mother be allowed to return. The request was granted, and Helena returned to Augsburg. She remained there, instructing seekers in the faith, until her death in 1545.

During her last years in Augsburg, Helena wrote a confession of her personal faith. This writing shows her deep personal faith and that Anabaptists practiced both discipline and forgiveness.

When she married, Helena von Freyberg lived at Hohenaschau Castle in Bavaria, Germany, where she raised her four sons.

Helena von Freyberg was interrogated by the authorities in Augsburg, Germany.

KATHERINE PRUST HUTTER (d. 1538)

Katherine Prust Hutter was from Taufers in the Puster Valley of the Tyrol. She likely learned about Anabaptism through working as a maid in a house associated with Anabaptists. She was baptized by Jacob Hutter, who later became her husband.

In 1534, Katherine joined a trek of Hutter's followers from the Puster region to Austerlitz. Prior to this, she had already been arrested twice for her Anabaptist identity. She married Jacob about May 1535.

Katherine was arrested a third time with her husband in 1535 in the Tyrol but escaped in early 1536. She remained in the Tyrol for two more years until she was arrested for the fourth and final time in the town of Schöneck.

URSULA JOST

Ursula Jost lived in the city of Strasbourg. In 1530, she published a forty-page book of apocalyptic visions. Apocalypticism is a view of the endtimes, usually involving some sort of cataclysmic clash. The social upheaval of the Reformation era and the relative tolerance of Strasbourg provided fertile ground for these apocalyptic visions to flourish. Some visions dealt with God's justice and vengeance against the wicked, while others called for patience until God would save the chosen people.

Anabaptist leader Melchior Hoffman read Jost's writings. Her prophetic visions reinforced his own. Hoffman became further convinced that he would have a key role in endtimes events. Jost was married to the butcher Lienhard Jost, who also had visions valued by Hoffman. Hoffman was more open to listening to a woman than were many religious leaders of his day.

ELIZABETH DIRKS (d. 1549)

Elizabeth Dirks is sometimes called the first Mennonite deaconess. As a young girl she had been sent to a convent where she learned to read Latin. When she heard about a person condemned to death because of his Anabaptist faith, she decided to read the scriptures herself to seek what had led him to that point. After a period of time, Elizabeth determined that she would leave the convent and seek out this community of Anabaptist believers. She escaped from the convent by borrowing clothes from one of the milkmaids who regularly came and went from the convent.

Upon leaving, she first went to the town of Leer. Later she became a leader of an Anabaptist congregation in Leeuwarden. *Martyrs Mirror* recorded her brave and faithful testimony, given under torture. She was condemned to death by drowning, on March 27, 1549.

What leadership roles do women in your ongregation or comunity hold?

Katherine Prust Hutter was baptized by Anabaptist leader Jacob Hutter, who later became her husband. Katherine was arrested, examined in Branzoll Castle (shown here), and later executed in 1538.

In 1558 an Anabaptist group was arrested at Aix-la-Chapelle. As recorded in *Martyrs Mirror*, the authorities even took with them "a mother with her infant that lay in the cradle." This Jan Luyken print displays the heart-rending scene.

"We have from the beginning of our ministry been ready and desirous to give an account of our faith to every person who asked it in good faith, whether they were ruler or citizen, learned or unlearned, rich or poor, man or woman."
—*Menno Simons*

What turning points in life have you experienced?

Elizabeth Soto Albrecht (in green), then Moderator of Mennonite Church USA, leads a prayer walk in downtown Phoenix in July of 2013, as part of the biennial convention.

Some WWII-era COs (conscientious objectors) served as smoke jumpers. This photo shows COs in Missoula, Montana, training under the direction of the U.S. Forest Service to fight forest fires. A jump from the training tower simulated jumping from a plane.

Nonviolence

SIXTEENTH-CENTURY POSITIONS

Anabaptists of the sixteenth century held a wide range of views regarding either rejection of violence or the use of violence. Though this may be surprising to modern-day Anabaptists who associate the word *Anabaptist* with nonviolence, it is helpful to remember that in the sixteenth century the word Anabaptist simply meant "baptism again" or "rebaptizer." As mentioned in previous chapters, Balthasar Hubmaier, Jan Matthijs, Jan van Leiden, and Bernhard Rothmann all defended use of the sword.

It is, however, nonviolent sixteenth-century Anabaptist thought that has carried forward into our present day. Michael Sattler included nonviolence as a principle in the *Schleitheim Articles*, the 1527 statement that became one of the defining texts for Swiss Anabaptists. A letter written by Conrad Grebel in September 1524 (and signed by Felix Mantz and others) outlined this position as well. Pilgram Marpeck, Jacob Hutter, and Menno Simons completely rejected the use of the sword. Dirk Willems, who turned back to save the life of his pursuer at the cost of his own, is an example of a sixteenth-century Anabaptist who lived out discipleship to Jesus by returning good for evil.

DISCIPLESHIP

A disciple is one who follows and learns at the feet of a master. Discipleship in Anabaptist theology is discipleship to Jesus. Anabaptists accept the teachings of Jesus and take the specifics of Jesus' life as the standard by which life will be measured. In other words, Anabaptists look at how Jesus acted, spoke, and lived, and try to follow that example. Readers of the Gospels see examples of Jesus crossing social, political, and economic boundaries to relate to people—stories such as Jesus talking to the Samaritan woman at the well (John 4), healing a man's withered hand on the Sabbath day (Matthew 12), and sharing meals with tax collectors (Luke 19).

definition

THE SWORD
A sword was a soldier's weapon before guns became common. The use of violence is therefore sometimes referred to as the use of the sword.

definition

Many words are used when discussing the use of the sword and the practice of nonviolence.

NONVIOLENCE

Nonviolence is the refusal to use violence.

NONRESISTANCE

Nonresistance is a principle based on a translation of Matthew 5:39, in which Jesus says to "resist not evil." Some people understand this command to mean "make no response." For example, those who hold to nonresistance would refuse to participate in the military but may also be hesitant to join a public protest. Instead, they allow their everyday practices to be a witness to the nonviolence of Jesus.

NONVIOLENT RESISTANCE

Nonviolent resistance is action-focused but uses only nonviolent methods to witness, or to bring about change. Recent advocates of peace and nonviolence use the passage beginning in Matthew 5:39 to suggest that "do not resist an evildoer" means "do not mirror evil" but instead use creative means to change the situation.

PACIFISM

Pacifism is a commitment to nonviolence. Specifically, it is a refusal to be part of the military. The term is especially relevant when describing times when governments require universal military service. Many pacifists are COs (conscientious objectors) who complete voluntary service assignments instead of serving military terms.

SERMON ON THE MOUNT

The Sermon on the Mount is found in the New Testament, in the book of Matthew, chapters 5 to 7. These spoken words of Jesus were written down and saved. In the Sermon on the Mount, Jesus compares the children of God to a light on a hill (Matthew 5:14). He urges his followers to live in a way that their lives display characteristics of God's Kingdom.

The Beatitudes are found in the Sermon on the Mount (Matthew 5:3-10).

Blessed are the poor in spirit, for theirs is the kingdom of heaven.
Blessed are those who mourn, for they will be comforted.
Blessed are the meek, for they will inherit the earth.
Blessed are those who hunger and thirst for righteousness, for they will be filled.
Blessed are the merciful, for they will receive mercy.
Blessed are the pure in heart, for they will see God.
Blessed are the peacemakers, for they will be called children of God.
Blessed are those who are persecuted for righteousness' sake, for theirs is the kingdom of heaven.

The painting "Peace Be Still," by Chinese Christian artist He Qi (www.heqiart.com), depicts the story of Jesus and his disciples in a storm-tossed boat (Mark 4:35-41).

" DO NOT RESIST AN EVILDOER"

These words from Matthew 5:39-48 are often used to discuss response to oppression:

> You have heard that it was said, 'An eye for an eye and a tooth for a tooth.' But I say to you, Do not resist an evildoer. But if anyone strikes you on the right cheek, turn the other also; and if anyone wants to sue you and take your coat, give your cloak as well; and if anyone forces you to go one mile, go also the second mile.

In this passage, Jesus is urging his followers to refrain from returning violence for violence and also suggests ways in which an oppressive situation might be changed. For example, in suggesting that a person should "go a second mile," it is important to know that at the time Jesus lived, it was a law that a Roman soldier could command a civilian to carry his 80-pound pack of military gear. However, military regulations forbade soldiers to force a civilian to carry the pack for more than a mile; a soldier could find himself in trouble if that occurred. Thus, a civilian who followed Jesus' suggestion might end up with the soldier begging him to put down the pack.

Jesus immediately follows these examples with, "Love your enemies." It shows that the ways of responding are not done to humiliate the oppressor but to expose the oppression and then to give the oppressor an opportunity to change.

THE WRITINGS OF PAUL

Paul is echoing these teachings of Jesus when he writes: "If your enemies are hungry, feed them; if they are thirsty, give them something to drink; for by doing this you will heap burning coals on their heads. Do not be overcome by evil, but overcome evil with good (Romans 12:20-21). In I Thessalonians 5:15 Paul writes, "See that none of you repays evil for evil, but always seek to do good to one another and to all."

In 2014, the Freeman (South Dakota) Network for Peace and Justice commissioned artist Michelle Hofer to design two banners based on Isaiah 11:6-9:

The wolf shall live with the lamb, the leopard shall lie down with the kid, the calf and the lion and the fatling together, and a little child shall lead them. The cow and the bear shall graze, their young shall lie down together; and the lion shall eat straw like the ox. The nursing child shall play over the hole of the asp, and the weaned child shall put its hand on the adder's den. They will not hurt or destroy on all my holy mountain; for the earth will be full of the knowledge of the Lord as the waters cover the sea.

HISTORIC PEACE CHURCHES
Mennonites, Brethren, and Quakers have often been identified as the historic peace churches. Members of these communities are traditionally pacifists, choosing voluntary service assignments in place of serving in the military during times of war. Hutterites and Amish also embrace a pacifist tradition.

PEACE WITNESS DURING TIMES OF WAR

Wars are often used as reference points when histories are written. The following section witnesses to people and voices calling for alternative paths during times of war. The stories here are specific to North America, beginning with the American revolution and approaching the contemporary era. It is important to acknowledge, however, that a survey such as this could be taken in many different places and time periods. It is also important to realize that a peace witness can, and should, extend beyond a consideration of whether or not to participate in war efforts. Equally significant are stories of individuals and communities working for social, racial, and economic justice.

The American Revolution

1775 was a time of fighting and tension in the American colonies. In particular, April 1775 saw battles in Lexington and Concord between British soldiers and Massachusetts patriots. In May of that year, patriots in each of the colonies drew up agreements that obligated all those who signed to begin military training to fight the British. As part of their expression of faith, Mennonites generally refused to join these associations or to train as soldiers.

Hostility was expressed by many of the patriots towards the Mennonites. In June 1778, ten Mennonite families from Upper Saucon were brought into court in Easton, Pennsylvania, because the men had refused to sign an affirmation that they would support the revolutionary cause through military participation. These ten families were told to leave the state within thirty days; all of their belongings were confiscated and sold, "even their Beds, Beddings, Linen, Bible & Books" and the "children's flour was taken out of the sack and even the women's spinning wheels."

In November 1775, Benjamin Hershey, a Lancaster County Mennonite leader, wrote *A Short and Sincere Declaration* outlining the Mennonite position of objection to military service. It was in response to a request that those who refused to participate in military service would instead pay an extra tax. Hershey wrote that this request would be acceptable if the contributions of nonresistants would be used exclusively for the relief of the poor, in that it was "our Principle to feed the hungry and give the Thirsty Drink." The Declaration went on to say that the non-resistants could not go beyond this for "we find no Freedom in giving, or doing, or assisting in any Thing by which Men's Lives are destroyed or hurt."

The Declaration was signed by Mennonites and Brethren.

Eine kurze und aufrichtige Erklärung/A Short and Sincere Declaration (1775) by Bishop Benjamin Hershey was published in both German and English and described the Mennonite beliefs about taxes during the U.S. Revolutionary War.

The American Civil War

This 1862 photo shows Sarah Bowman and Catharine Showalter carrying provisions to Brethren imprisoned for refusing to perform military service. (Harrisonburg, Virginia)

What stories of peace witness are important to you?

Some COs during World War I agreed to wear the military uniform and others did not. Of these COs in the state of Washington in 1918, there were four known Mennonites. Orie Conrad (middle row, far right) refused to train or wear the uniform. He was nearly hanged but saved by his commanding officer. Conrad's tormentors were court-martialed.

World War I

During World War I, conscientious objectors (COs) experienced a variety of reactions from neighbors, community members and local governments. Some COs were respected, or at least tolerated, for their positions. Others received rough treatment at the hands of local authorities, vigilante groups, or officials in charge of military camps. Some COs chose to appease local resentment by buying liberty bonds or displaying the American flag. Historian James Juhnke tells the story of Bernhard Harder, a leader of Emmaus Mennonite Church, near Whitewater, Kansas. A mob arrived at Harder's farmhouse, intent upon harm. Harder turned aside the angry men by suggesting that they all sing "America" together. Harder led off in a loud and vigorous voice. Though the others were able to join in on the first verse, Harder alone knew the words to verses two, three, and four, and so finished the patriotic hymn by himself. Shortly thereafter, the crowd dispersed.

... the whole congregation to my Father and Mother in law. especially send this letter to my Brothers at Magreth Albertas and to cousin Peter J. Hofer. Storebock Manitoba.

in God to the End.   Your sorrowful Son

Jacob J. Wipf.

A Prisoner for Consience sake.

Portion of a letter sent from prison, by Jacob Wipf to his parents.

Grave markers in South Dakota for the two Hutterite brothers who died in military custody, linked to the Anabaptist martyr tradition.

MICHAEL HOFER – MARTYR
1893 – 1918

JOSEPH HOFER – MARTYR
1894 – 1918

A particularly tragic story comes from the Rockport Bruderhof, a Hutterite community in South Dakota. In 1918, four young men— Joseph, Michael, and David Hofer (brothers) and their brother-in-law Jacob Wipf— of the Bruderhof were required to report for military duty in Lewis, Washington. However, upon arrival at the military camp, they refused to wear military clothing or participate in the military exercises, holding fast to a position of nonviolence as a reflection of their religious convictions. They were thrown into a prison cell for two months, at which point they received their sentence: thirty-seven years in prison (later reduced to twenty), to be served on the island of Alcatraz. Over the next several months, they were beaten, received little food or water, and were forced to stand for long periods of time with their hands chained to steel posts over their heads. After four months they were transferred to Fort Leavenworth in Kansas. They reached their destination at 11:00 pm and were driven down the middle of the streets at bayonet point. Joseph and Michael Hofer were transferred to a hospital, unable to function any longer. Jacob and David were again put into cells.

On November 29, 1918, Joseph Hofer died, and military officials dressed him in uniform before putting him in his coffin. Michael died a few days later, on December 2. David was released shortly thereafter. One hundred and thirteen COs were released from Fort Leavenworth on January 27, 1919. Jacob Wipf was released on April 13th.

World War II

By World War II, the position of conscientious objection was recognized, and COs were granted permission to refuse military service and instead perform civil service. COs during World War II worked in mental health hospitals, as forest fire smoke jumpers, and on park and trail restoration. On Vancouver Island (Canada), seventeen million trees were planted in two years. A British

Alcatraz prison in the early 1900s.

Many but not all Canadian Mennonite men of draft age during World War II chose to enter the alternative service program as COs. In 1945 there were about 1,600 COs in British Columbia. They often worked in rural areas and parks—doing maintenance, fire fighting, planting seedlings, and other forest work.

What peacemakers are active in your congregation or community today?

Columbia forestry official stated, "The ASWs [Alternative Service Workers] are the best forest fighters we ever had." Over 3000 COs worked in mental health hospitals in twenty-three states. The presence of these COs helped bring to light the deplorable conditions and inhumane treatment given many of the patients.

Some women chose to join voluntary service units alongside the men who were performing alternative service assignments. Calling themselves "CO Girls," one of these units was placed in a mental health hospital in Cleveland in the summer of 1945. Gladys Graber Beyler, a new graduate of Goshen College, was a member of this group. She remembers that the unit arrived on the women's ward at suppertime and realized that none of the patients had utensils for eating. The head of their unit, Dr. Luella Smith (then professor at Bethel College), went to the doctors in charge and requested that spoons be given the patients. The following day, spoons were allowed, though the CO Girls had to count them after each meal. Gladys also remembers women patients who had lost the use of their arms from being kept in straitjackets for so long.

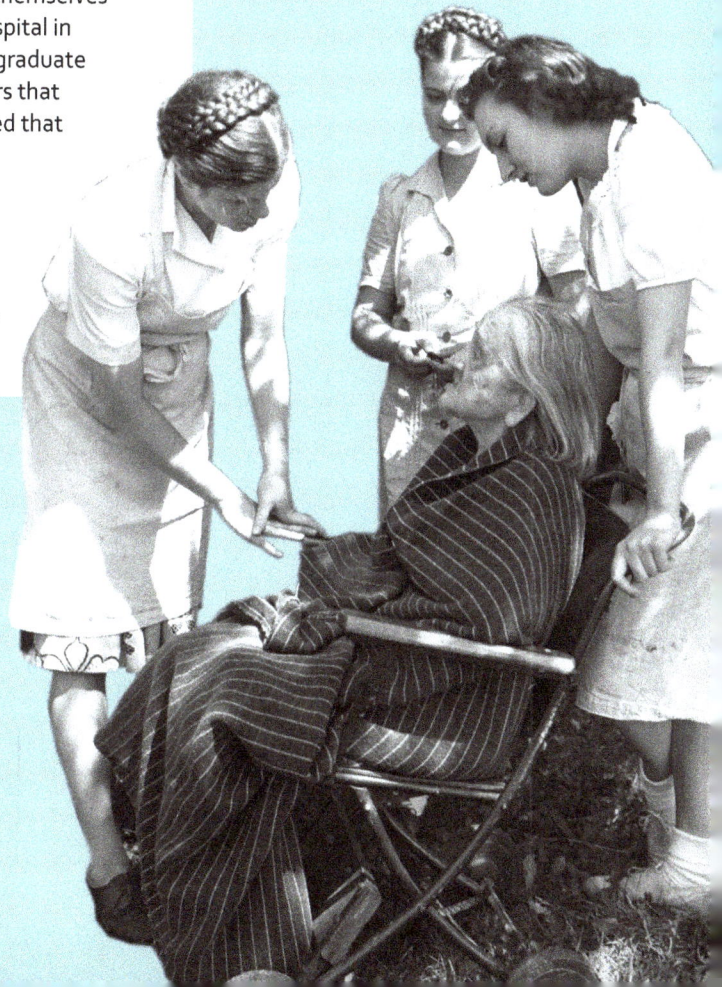

CPS Camp #69, Cleveland, Ohio, 1945-46. Gladys Graber Beyler (left) and two other CO Girls assist an elderly patient at Cleveland State Hospital in Ohio.

CO Girl Guidelines

The CO Girls wrote a set of guidelines for themselves, to shape their time in the hospitals:

1 Speak a greeting to anyone, everyone on the hospital campus, in the corridors, on the wards, in the cafeteria.

2 Be willing to do any task regardless of how menial or filthy.

3 Be willing to mingle and eat with others in the dining room.

4 Discuss first with your ward attendants any concerns you may have about unsatisfactory conditions.

5 Be at anytime ready to give witness to what you believe.

Sarah Thompson became the Executive Director of Christian Peacemaker Teams in January 2014. A 2011 graduate of Anabaptist Mennonite Biblical Seminary, Sarah first learned of CPT while participating in Peace Club at Bethany Christian High School in Goshen, Indiana.

"It will take an expanding worldwide but grassroots culture reaching beyond national borders to fashion a body of Christian peacemeakers to be an effective power to block guns and be part of transforming each impending tragedy of war."

Gene Stoltzfus,
1940-2010

Vietnam War Era

Many young men performed overseas assignments with Mennonite Central Committee, in place of serving in the military. These MCC assignments involved varied tasks, such as teaching in schools, health care in refugee camps, and agricultural and water development projects.

Other young Mennonite men found that their faith convictions led them to resist the military draft altogether. These young men refused to register with the Selective Service and often faced jail terms.

Christian Peacemaker Teams

Going only where invited by local peacemakers, Christian Peacemaker Teams (CPT) work alongside communities experiencing lethal conflict as a result of structural injustice. CPT members seek to be a visible, peaceful presence and witness. CPT was started in 1986, with Gene Stoltzfus as the first director. CPT members were present in Iraq at the time of the US-led bombing of Baghdad in 2003 and continue in the northern region of Iraq today. They also focus on undoing oppressions as a key element of peacemaking.

CPT member Weldon Nisley was seriously injured in a car accident while in Iraq. Upon reaching the hospital (which had been bombed three days earlier by American military forces), the Iraqi ambulance driver carried Weldon in his arms for the final steps from vehicle to door. In later written reflections, Weldon remembers the ambulance driver as 'being the face of Jesus' to him, and asks, "When we meet people who are desperate for help, who need a neighbor, will we be there?" (Seasoned With Peace , Winter)

STORIES OF GLOBAL ANABAPTIST PEACEMAKERS

JUSTA PAZ, COLOMBIA

In 2014, members of the Colombian Mennonite organization Justa Paz demonstrated their support for South Korean conscientious objector San-Ming Lee. Lee, the first Mennonite in South Korea to declare himself a CO, is serving an 18-month jail sentence for his religious convictions. Justa Paz has been active in Colombia for almost twenty-five years, supporting young men from around the country who choose to object to Colombia's compulsory military service. Justa Paz advocates for the inclusion of CO status in Colombia's legal system and also organizes workshops and theological training to promote nonviolent peacebuilding.

RETURN TO THE EARTH PROJECT, UNITED STATES

Lawrence Hart, born in 1933 in Oklahoma, became a Cheyenne Peace Chief and a Mennonite minister. He initiated and helped organize Return to the Earth, a peace, justice, and reconciliation project supported by Mennonite Central Committee's Restorative Justice office. Return to the Earth seeks to provide dignified burials for the thousands of remains of Native American peoples that are currently housed on museum shelves throughout North America.

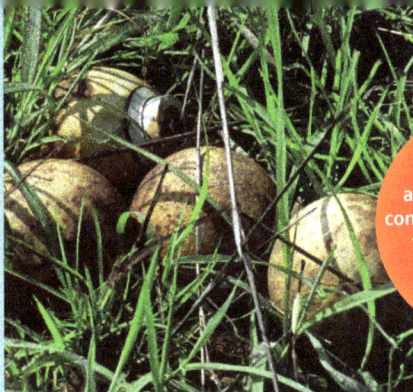

How can you, as an individual or congregation, witness to peace in your community?

MENNONITE CENTRAL COMMITTEE, LAOS

Nearly 80 million unexploded bomblets (tennisball sized explosives) lie in the fields of Laos. They are a sobering reminder of US military air strikes during the Vietnam War era. Decades later, families experience tragedy anew when adults and children working in gardens and fields inadvertently set off the bomblets while digging or hoeing. Mennonite Central Committee (MCC) workers have been involved with bomblet removal for many years; recent MCC work has focused on advocating for an international ban on the use of cluster bombs.

JAPAN MENNONITE OBIHIRO CHRISTIAN CHURCH, JAPAN

Every Sunday, members of Japan Mennonite Obihiro Christian Church read together the following confession of faith, adopted in May of 2013 by the Japan Mennonite Christian Church Conference (Hokkaido):

- *Jesus Christ is the Word of God the Father, and is revealed by the Holy Spirit.*

- *The church is a community of believers, which learns from the Bible under the guidance of the Holy Spirit.*

- *Believers listen to the Lord Jesus Christ, serve each other, and love their neighbors.*

- *Believers care for creation; build peace and justice, which come from Christ; and participate in the work of the kingdom of God.*

- *Following Jesus' nonviolent way of life, we as believers do not participate in war.*

Children surround a Youth Venture team leader at a summer Bible camp at First Mennonite Church and Primera Iglesia Menonita in Reedley, California. (2010)

Anabaptists in North America Today

MENNONITES, HUTTERITES, AMISH, BRETHREN

The first nine chapters of this book examine sixteenth-century Anabaptist beginnings. This chapter will look specifically at the modern-day structures of North American Anabaptists. Readers should be aware, however, that this brief survey is only that—a general overview designed to pique interest, raise questions, and encourage further exploration and sharing of faith histories. In addition, the authors emphasize that the Anabaptist community extends well beyond modern-day North American borders; the rich diversity of the global Anabaptist community is cause for additional study and inspiration.

NORTH AMERICAN DENOMINATIONS

In North America, Mennonites, Hutterites, Amish, and Brethren are the four largest Anabaptist denominations today. There are, however, other groups with Anabaptist roots and connections, including the Brethren in Christ, Apostolic Christian Church, and the Bruderhof communities.

The **Brethren in Christ** movement began in Lancaster County, Pennsylvania, in 1780, by Anabaptists (mostly Mennonites) who were drawn to the idea of crisis conversion. Crisis conversion is the belief that individuals experience salvation at a specific moment in time; at the start of the movement, the conversion experience was often connected to a revival meeting. Brethren in Christ today have a strong missionary orientation. Messiah College in Grantham, Pennsylvania, was founded by the Brethren in Christ.

After he was expelled from the Swiss Reformed Church, Samuel Frölich founded the **Apostolic Christian Church** in 1832 at Langnau, Switzerland. Frölich's followers included previous members of the Reformed Church as well as dissatisfied Anabaptists. Frölich emphasized adult baptism, a clear personal faith, and rejection of military service. Today the Apostolic Christian Church has congregations in two groups in the United States and many congregations in eastern Europe.

The **Bruderhof** were founded in Germany in 1920 by Eberhard Arnold. The Bruderhof live in community, much like Hutterites. Today there are Bruderhof communities in New York, Pennsylvania, West Virginia, and Florida in the United States, as well as in Germany, the United Kingdom, Paraguay, and Australia. For a time, because of similar outlooks, the Bruderhof were affiliated with Hutterites.

What are the blessings and challenges of living in community?

Hutterites at the Silverwind Colony in Manitoba, Canada, listen to their young children.

HUTTERITES

The Hutterites carry the name of Jacob Hutter, a sixteenth-century Anabaptist leader in Moravia. The Hutterites are known for their practice of community of goods—the sharing and owning of all things in common.

The Hutterite communities experienced terrible persecution from Archduke Ferdinand from 1534 to 1537. It is likely that knowledge of the violent Anabaptist kingdom in Münster contributed to public opinion against the Anabaptists in Moravia, even though the Moravian Anabaptists were mostly peaceful. Many Anabaptists were executed in Moravia during this time period; many others fled.

After 1540 conditions began to improve for those Hutterites remaining in Moravia. From about 1565 to 1595, Hutterites enjoyed a period of prosperity in

Moravia. This has been called their "Golden Age." In this period, they became known for their skilled work; their handcrafted pottery, knives and cutting instruments were recognized widely. The Hutterites developed hygienic and medical practices that were much advanced for that time, and their doctors were in demand outside their colonies as well as within.

The devastation of the Thirty Years War (1618-48), however, eliminated virtually all Hutterite presence in Moravia. Some were killed; others moved to what is now Romania and eventually to the southern part of the Russian Empire at the invitation of Catherine the Great (alongside Mennonites of Dutch descent). The practice of community of goods lapsed in this time of transition. However, the practice was revived in Russia, and was brought to North America when Hutterites began to emigrate in 1874.

The Hutterites settled primarily in the prairie states and provinces of the United States and Canada and are still thriving today, keeping their communities separate from the mainstream society. Hutterites live on large farms, which they operate collectively. Electricity and modern equipment—such as machinery and appliances—can be found in barns, fields and homes. Tasks are divided among community members. Meals are eaten together in a large dining hall. Each family has individual sleeping quarters, but personal property is minimal. Women and girls wear dresses and often wear polka-dotted headscarves.

There are three different Hutterite groups. They carry the name of the leader or the leader's profession at the time of immigration to North America. The Schmiedeleut are named for their first leader, Michael Waldner who was a blacksmith. S*chmiede* means blacksmith and *leut* means people in the Hutterite dialect of German. The Schmiedeleut have colonies in Minnesota, North and South Dakota, and Manitoba. The Dariusleut are named for Darius Walter. They live in Montana, Washington, Alberta, Saskatchewan, and British Columbia. Jakob Wipf, a teacher, was the first leader of the Lehrerleut. *Lehrer* means teacher. Their colonies are found in Montana, Alberta, and Saskatchewan. Some cultural patterns differ among these groups.

Hutterites speak a German dialect. It can be called Hutterisch. Their sermons, almost always read from their large collection of old, written sermons, are in old High German (early High German).

Hutterite children in school (above). Hutterites have large farming colonies in rural areas (below).

Amish buggies can often be seen on roadways in Lancaster County, Pennsylvania.

AMISH

The Amish carry the name of Jakob Ammann, a seventeenth-century Swiss Anabaptist leader. Ammann was likely born in 1644 and was a tailor by trade. He joined the Anabaptists in 1670 and was later ordained as a minister. Ammann had strong feelings about the importance of spiritual renewal among the Swiss (Brethren) Anabaptists. He prohibited attendance at state church services, encouraged untrimmed beards for men, and called for the practice of shunning (the social exclusion of community members who break community rules). Shunning is an element of church discipline, advocated in several biblical passages, and intended to help members recognize their error and return to the community.

The specific division between the Amish and other Mennonites occurred in 1693 in Switzerland and the Alsace region of contemporary France. Hans Reist was the leader of those who remained with the traditional ways and continued to use the name Swiss Brethren, and later Mennonite.

Amman introduced foot-washing in worship; this would have been a new practice for Swiss Anabaptists of the time. Like other Anabaptists of that place and time, Ammann was opposed to participation in the military. In February of 1696, Ammann signed a petition protesting compulsory military service.

The Swiss and Alsace Anabaptist refugees who came to North America beginning in the early eighteenth century included Amish. In North America, the Amish were first known as Amish Mennonites, though over time they dropped the name *Mennonite*.

In the United States, before the development of automobiles and electricity, Mennonites and Amish resembled each other and had few theological differences except for the Mennonite use of meeting houses for worship and the Amish practice of shunning. Both Mennonites and Amish had a variety of responses to the development of modern technology and the opportunities offered by higher education. The Amish churches that accepted modern developments eventually merged with assimilated Mennonites who also accepted these changes. The Amish who chose not to own automobiles, install telephones in home, and attend schools of higher education, but rather desired to maintain traditional practices including plain clothing styles became known as the Old Order Amish in the 1870s.

So called "plain dress" for women included black bonnets and cape dresses of solid, darker colors. A cape dress has an additional cloth panel over the bust. Men wear simple shirts and frock coats without buttons for church services. Old Order Amish use horses and buggies for transportation and work their fields with teams of horses. This profile of the Amish is often the image held by the general public when the name *Amish* is used.

The Old Order Amish do not reject certain forms of technology, such as the car or television, because they believe these are intrinsically evil. Instead, they fear such products will destroy their family and the community-based way of life that they cherish. They believe that God has blessed this way of life and want to preserve it as much as possible.

In the United States until recently, most Old Order Amish were farmers. Now more than half of them work in small businesses such as buggy making, machine shops, wood-working and furniture-making, craft shops, and retail stores that offer their wares to their own people as well as the larger society. A few work in non-Amish factories that build various products, such as mobile homes in northern Indiana. North America's Amish population of ca. 250,000 live in 28 states and Ontario. Well-known Amish areas are Lancaster, Pennsylvania, northern Indiana, and Holmes and Wayne counties in Ohio.

The Amish have preserved their German dialect, often called Pennsylvania Dutch. Martin Luther's translation of the Bible in German is read in church services. These services are held in homes every other Sunday. Conversation and preaching is in the German-derived dialect (Pennsylvania German as well as Swiss German.)

Each Amish community follows a local *Ordnung*, a set of unwritten rules that guide the daily life and practice of individuals within the congregation. The *Ordnung* holds members accountable to each other and sets standards for clothing style, transportation, work, and home life.

In what ways are members of Amish communities portrayed in popular media?

The fruit symbol on the Mack seal is a reference to Matthew 12:33. *Either make the tree good, and its fruit good; or make the tree bad, and its fruit bad; for the tree is known by its fruit.*

ALEXANDER MACK (1679-1735)
Mack was baptized as a baby in the Reformed Church of Schriesheim in the Palatinate in South Germany. His parents were relatively well-off, profiting from the family-owned mill. Mack's parents were active locally in both religious and political affairs.

Mack married Anna Margarethe Kling on January 18, 1701. Both Mack and his wife became active in the Pietist movement. They were devoted followers of Pietist leader Ernst Christoph Hochmann von Hochenau. Mack did some traveling with Hochmann, on speaking and teaching trips.

Mack also began holding illegal Bible studies in his home. After a high law enforcement officer broke up a worship service in Mack's home, he and Anna took what belongings they could carry and fled from Schriesheim. Eventually they settled in the small village of Schwarzenau, located in the religiously tolerant county of Wittgenstein, Germany. Mack continued to travel with Hochmann.

CHURCH OF THE BRETHREN

The Brethren movement began in Schwarzenau, Germany, in 1708. The original five men and three women first baptized into the movement were primarily from the Reformed Church in the Palatinate. Alexander Mack was the first minister of the Brethren movement.

Distinct characteristics of the Brethren include: the belief that there should be no creed but the New Testament, which is the guide to daily living; baptism done by immersing the individual three times; the understanding that church and state should be separate; no taking of oaths; no bearing of arms; the practice of celebrating communion as a Love Feast (a congregational meal); baptism and the Love Feast are the ordinances (sacred practices) of the church; and the use of council meetings to determine church governance.

The Brethren were shaped by both Anabaptism and Pietism. Pietism is a movement that originated in Germany in the late seventeenth century, as a reaction to the strong emphasis placed on doctrine (rules and laws) found in Reformed and Lutheran traditions. Pietist thought emphasized the emotional and heartfelt response to the message of the gospel. Pietists did not disagree with the classic doctrines but insisted that mere belief in doctrine was not enough, shifting the emphasis to a heartfelt expression of Jesus as savior. The Pietist movement revealed itself in various ways, depending on location and leadership.

In their early years, Brethren were sometimes called *Neu Täufer* (New Baptists) to distinguish them from Mennonites and Swiss Brethren, whom they closely resembled. They were formally known as the German Baptist Brethren but eventually received nicknames in North America such as Dunkers and Dunkards. These names came from the practice of baptism by immersion.

Many Brethren immigrated to North America in two groups in 1719 and 1729. By 1733 virtually all the Brethren had immigrated to North America.

Mack sometimes visited Mennonite communities on his teaching and preaching missions; these Mennonite communities would have practiced adult baptism. As well, pietist gatherings in Schwarzenau often discussed baptism. In the summer of 1708, two visitors (likely associated with Mennonites) came through Schwarzenau and urged Mack to practice adult baptism, in spite of its illegality. After much Bible study, prayer, and discussion, eight persons chose adult baptism in the first week of August 1708. The eight were baptized in the Eder River that flows through Schwarzenau. One person was chosen by lot to baptize Mack and he baptized the others.

This group of eight became an organized congregation, called the New Baptists of Schwarzenau. Alexander Mack was their leader. These Brethren established beliefs that are still accepted by the Brethren today.

These moves took place at the same time as many other German settlers, including Mennonites.

The German Baptist Brethren experienced a three-way division in the early 1880s. A tradition-minded group known as the Old German Baptist Brethren separated from the main body, which kept the name German Baptist Brethren. About the same time a change-minded group, known as the Brethren Church, also parted ways. Eventually in 1908 the large main body changed its name from German Baptist Brethren to Church of the Brethren. This is still the largest of the Brethren denominations. In 1926, the very conservative Dunkard Brethren left the Church of the Brethren to form a separate church.

The Church of the Brethren exists worldwide through independent churches in Nigeria, India, Brazil, Dominican Republic, Haiti, and Spain. Many churches in India that were products of Brethren missionaries have joined the church of North India.

Within the change-minded Brethren Church in the 1920s and 1930s, a movement emerged that was shaped by the Fundamentalist movement. This movement led to the formation of the fundamentalist Fellowship of Grace Brethren Churches (Winona Lake, Indiana), which had a high view of the inspiration of scripture, and a stress on the premillennial view of eschatology. Premillennialists believe that Jesus will return to earth and rule his kingdom on earth for one thousand years before the final judgement. Grace Brethren emphasize a mission outlook and are active in many countries around the world.

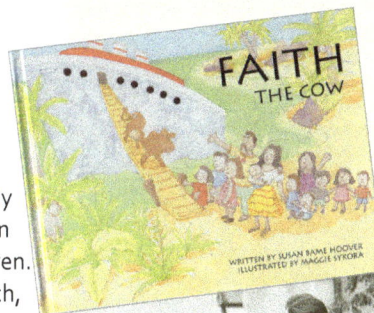

FAITH THE COW
WRITTEN BY SUSAN BAME HOOVER
ILLUSTRATED BY MAGGIE SYKORA

DAN WEST AND THE COWS
Heifer International is a global organization dedicated to providing families with sustainable food and income sources. It was started by Dan West, a Church of the Brethren service worker. Dan West, right, presents cattle as part of the "Heifer Project" he envisioned. Farmers in Dan West's home congregation sent cows to families in Puerto Rico in 1944. The story of Dan West is told in the picture book *Faith the Cow* by Susan Bame Hoover.

What does it mean to have "No creed but the Bible"?

This footwashing service at Kulp Bible College in Kwarhi, Nigeria, was followed with a Love Feast and communion. The juice for communion was made out of strawberries. The school is operated by the Nigerian Church of the Brethren.

"We Are Able" workcampers serve on the campus of the Brethren Service Center, New Windsor, Maryland.

With main offices in New Windsor, Maryland, the Brethren Service Center offers support around the world in the areas of relief and development, disaster response, social justice, peace education, and hospitality. One organization of the Brethren Service Center is Brethren Disaster Ministries, which focuses on rebuilding homes and caring for children whose families have been impacted by natural disasters.

MENNONITES

Old Order, Conservative, and Change-Minded Mennonites

Changes that occurred in the the mid-nineteenth century produced two general clusters of North American Mennonites: tradition-minded ones, and change-minded (or assimilated) ones. Tradition-minded Mennonites would be those often

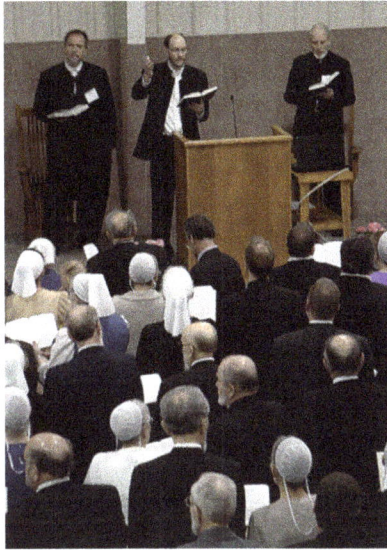

called Old Order or Conservative Mennonites and are most easily identified by outsiders. This is due to their choices of plain dress (which may include coverings for women and girls), transportation, and school and work patterns.

Old Order and Conservative Mennonites desire to maintain the local church community as the primary religious and social identity. These Mennonites reject much of modern culture and technology and prefer to maintain a traditional, rural way of life. This outlook is not simply a resistance to technology per se but reflects a concern that technology can undercut the strength of a local community. Television would be seen as detracting from family interactions. The use of cars would enable an individual to leave the community easily and seek resources and relationships elsewhere. Power tools create shortcuts that lessen the importance of cooperation and mutual assistance. In instances in which acceptance of technology is made, ownership and use of the technology may be governed by group expectations.

Old Order and Conservative Mennonites usually do not pursue higher education. Mennonites in these communities may establish their own schools for their children and young people. In the mid-nineteenth century, other changes considered progressive (and thus to be avoided) would have included the formation of Sunday schools, the holding of revival meetings, organization of missionary work, starts of Mennonite periodicals and publishing companies, and the beginnings of Mennonite colleges and national conferences.

In the year 2015, there were around 375,000 North American Mennonites. This number is difficult to establish, however, due to the multiple conferences that exist, the fact that some congregations do not belong to conferences, and the uneven practice of counting (some numbers may include children, while others include only baptized adults.) Nonetheless, it could be said that about half of these Mennonites hold an Old Order or Conservative Mennonite identity.

A partial listing of Conservative Mennonite affiliations would include the following: Conservative Mennonite Conference, Mid-Atlantic Mennonite Conference, Eastern Pennsylvania Mennonite Church, Church of God in Christ, Mennonite (Holdeman), and the National Mennonite Fellowship. MC USA is the largest North American Mennonite structure, with membership of approximately 95,000 in 2015. In 2015, MC Canada membership was listed at 31,000. The Mennonite Brethren have about 38,000 members in Canada and 31,000 in the US.

Beachy Amish Mennonites generally require their members to wear similar clothing—to show their identiity and uniformity.

Worship at Home Street Mennonite Church, Winnipeg, Manitoba.

Members of Aposento Alto Iglesia Menonita (Upper Room Mennonite Church) in Wichita, Kansas.

Sudanese Mennonite immigrants in Edmonton, Alberta.

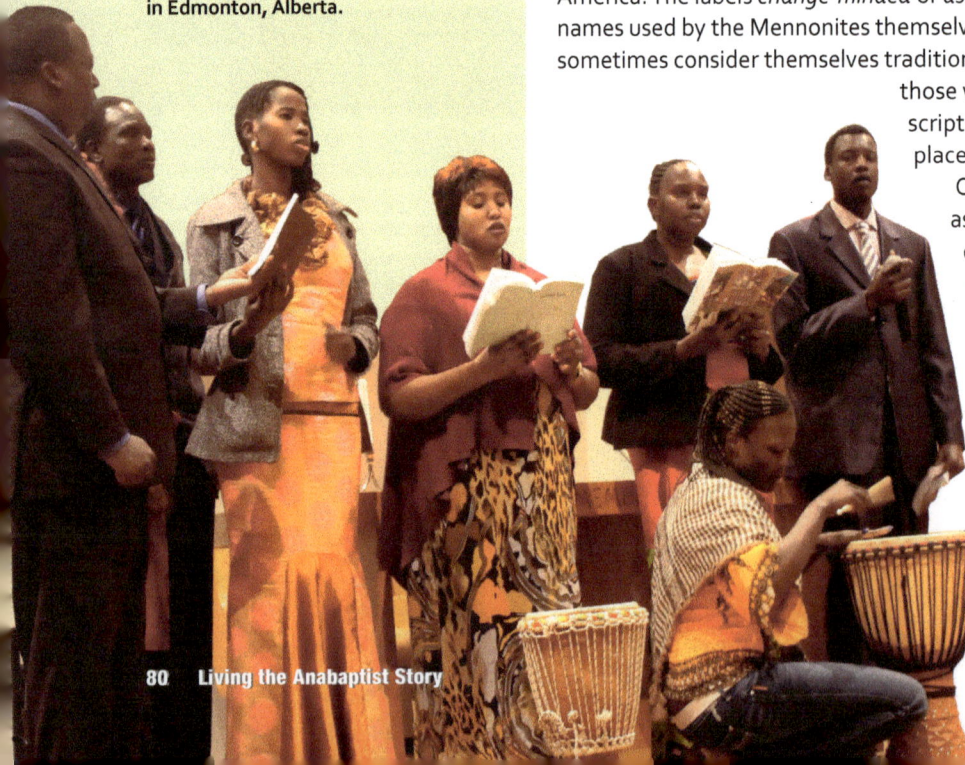

Change-minded (or assimilated) Mennonites is a description of those who are more fully integrated into the larger society. Examples of integration would include holding college and graduate degrees and working outside of rural settings. Clothing style may not immediately identify an individual as Mennonite, though certain options, such as camouflage pants or patriotic symbols, may be avoided. Modern electrical appliances (dishwashers, computers) would be found in homes and individuals would own and drive cars.

Based on this description, many though by no means all individuals, congregations, and member organizations in Mennonite Church Canada (MC Canada) or Mennonite Church USA (MC USA), could be identified as change-minded or assimilated Mennonites. This would be true as well for Mennonite Brethren, which began in southern Russia in 1860, but later immigrated to North America. The labels *change-minded* or *assimilated*, however, are not often names used by the Mennonites themselves who fit the category and who may sometimes consider themselves traditional according to markers other than those we are highlighting; rather, it is a description that identifies a division that took place in the mid-nineteenth century.

Outward signs may provide some clue as to where along the wide continuum of Mennonites (from traditional to change-minded) an individual or congregation finds itself. It is significant to note, however, that these attitudes of tradition, change, and assimilation are flexible and subject to discussion. The difference between one position and another is not always clear. In addition, individuals and congregations joining have joined MC Canada and MC USA in recent decades have contributed

"Black Mennonite Women Rock" weekend at Camp Friedenswald (Michigan), organized by Pastor Cyneatha Millsaps of Community Mennonite Church, Markham, Illinois. (Mennonite Women retreat, Sept. 2014)

different faith histories and diverse cultural, theological, and worship expressions. Congregations whose members have recently emigrated from other places, or who hold identities distinct from the dominant culture, will have a wide variety of expectations, hopes, fears, and ideas about what it means to assimilate or be separate from the society that surrounds them.

MC Canada and MC USA

At the beginning of the twenty-first century (2000-2001), a merger between the two largest North American Mennonite denominations (the Mennonite Church and the General Conference Mennonite Church) resulted in major restructuring along country boundaries. In simple terms, it could be said that these two large bodies merged and then re-divided along national boundaries. This was the start of MC Canada and MC USA, both of which identify themselves as national denominations.

In contrast to Old Order and Conservative Mennonite communities, many individuals and congregations in MC Canada and MC USA hold faith stories which begin in times and places other than sixteenth-century Europe. Many Mennonite churches have formed in urban settings that previously had no Mennonite presence. Some of these congregations are shaped by a particular language or cultural identity. In some urban contexts, such as Philadelphia where Mennonites first arrived over three centuries ago, racial-ethnic groups new to

Members of Buffalo Chin Emmanuel Church traveled for more than three hours to pray at the bedside of a critically injured conference member; a reunion photo was taken in October 2014, at the New York Mennonite Conference annual assembly.

Mennonites offered an expression of reconciliation to their Aboriginal neighbors at the Truth and Reconciliation Commission's sixth National Event, Sept. 18-21, 2013 in Vancouver.

How has social media and the Internet influenced your faith practices?

the Mennonite tradition are offering fresh vision and vitality. This is evident as Vietnamese, Indonesian, and other groups nurture flourishing congregations. Specific events (such as Native Assembly gatherings) and the creation of constituency groups (such as the African American Mennonite Association and *Iglesia Menonita Hispana*) give voice to individuals and communities within the two national structures of MC Canada and MC USA. Programs led by Mennonite Women and Mennonite Men exist in each of the two national bodies.

Areas of Disagreement

There are a variety of areas which, in past and present, have caused disagreements. At times these disagreements lead to divisions within congregations, conferences, and denominations. Examples of discussions include whether women should hold church leadership positions and the question of church membership for people who have divorced and remarried. In recent years, there has been significant conversation in MC Canada and MC USA about the membership, marriage, and ministry of Christians who are lesbian, gay, bisexual, or transgender. Individuals, families, congregations, conferences, and denominations have experienced the turmoil of living with fiercely defended, differing beliefs and alternate understandings of what it means to be a faithful, practicing, disciple of Jesus. In 2015 MC USA and its area conferences went through a number of discussions and changes of which the final outcome will not be known for a number of years. It is assumed that readers of this text will reflect a wide spectrum of thought on these topics.

Social Media and the Internet

Though the specifics may vary, Mennonites across the spectrum are affected by the recent, dramatic increase of Internet-connected devices in the world today. Individuals, families and congregations struggle with questions of how businesses operate and how people relate to one another. For example, a Conservative Mennonite community that has always avoided participation in the Internet may be faced with dilemmas of how a cabinet maker can remain in business if clients expect to communicate via email or websites. Is it okay for the Internet to be used for business purposes but not at home? Mennonites who accept and use electronic media without question in their homes may nonetheless struggle with how to help their children hear the words of Jesus amidst the ever-present voices of social media.

Relief Organizations

Mennonite Central Committee (MCC) began in the 1920s as a response to the civil war and famine that existed in southern Russia, where Mennonites lived. Today MCC works around the globe in disaster relief, peace and justice projects, and sustainable community development. MCC draws support from diverse Anabaptist groups throughout North America. Likewise, Mennonite Disaster Service (MDS), which serves communities devastated by natural disasters, is a cooperative effort sustained by individuals and congregations from many different branches of Anabaptists. Christian Aid Ministries (CAM), founded in 1981, is supported by Amish, Mennonites, and other conservative Anabaptist groups. With main offices in Berlin, Ohio, CAM tends to physical and spiritual needs around the globe.

Mennonite Disaster Service (MDS) responds in times of crisis, helping families and communities rebuild after tornadoes, floods, and other devastating events. Active supporters and volunteers come from many branches of Mennonites as well as other Anabaptist groups.

Mennonite World Conference

Worldwide Mennonites number nearly one and two-thirds million. The global Mennonite community includes congregations in all continents of the world except Antarctica. Countries with large numbers of Mennonites include the Congo, Ethiopia, Korea, India, Paraguay, Argentina, and Mexico. These congregations reflect the cultures of the countries in which they reside; this identity is expressed through style of worship, use of language and music, and expectations for personal and community interactions. In Europe there are present-day Mennonite congregations in Germany, Switzerland, and the Netherlands—the three countries in which Anabaptism emerged in the sixteenth century. Every six years, the Mennonite World Conference meets for a week of worship, workshops, sharing, and relationship-building.

Members of the 2015 Global Youth Summit planning committee.

Conclusion

Both newcomers and long-time heritage holders are keepers of the faith. Stories from the past can act as a rudder that keeps us pointed in a peace direction. We live in the present, bearing witness to the world of God's reign on earth. Newcomers, and in particular youth, have an opportunity to bring a fresh burst of enthusiasm and a glimpse of what is to come. As sisters and brothers in a global Anabaptist community, we are all responsible for exploring the past, acting in the present, and shaping the future.

explore
the past

act in the
present

shape
the future

1516
Erasmus publishes New Testament in Greek

1517
Martin Luther posts his 95 Theses in Wittenberg

1518
Ulrich Zwingli arrives in Zurich and begins preaching through the New Testament

1522
Andreas Castelberger begins Bible reading group, using Greek New Testament

1523
Zurich Disputation makes decision to reject papal authority and makes Zwingli head of the church in Zurich

Zurich Disputation rejects mass and icons; Conrad Grebel disappointed with pace of reform activity

Zurich Disputation affirms infant baptism

1525
January 21, 1525, first adult baptisms, in home of Anna Mantz

Peasants' War in Germany

Pilgram Marpeck leaves government office in Rattenberg and joins Anabaptists

1526
After being expelled from Waldshut, Balthasar Hubmaier arrives in Nikolsburg

1527
The noble woman Helena Von Freyberg is baptized as Anabaptist; leader of a congregation at Münichau

January 5, 1527, Felix Mantz is drowned in Limmat River in Zurich for the "crime" of rebaptizing

Schleitheim Articles edited by Michael Sattler in February; Michael Sattler burned at the stake on May 20

1528
Stäbler expelled from Nikolsburg; eventually establish at Austerlitz and retain community of goods

1500

timeline

6 "Blessed are those who hunger and thirst for righteousness, for they will be filled.

7 "Blessed are the merciful, for they will receive mercy.

8 "Blessed are the pure in heart, for they will see God.

9 "Blessed are the peacemakers, for they will be called children of God.

10 "Blessed are those who are persecuted... for theirs is...

...never enter the kingdom of heaven.

Concerning Anger

21 "You have heard that it was said to those of ancient times, 'You shall not murder'; and 'Whoever murders shall be liable to judgment.' But I say to you that if you are angry with a brother or sister, you will be liable to judgment; and if you insult a brother or sister, you will be liable to the council; and if you say 'You fool,' you will be liable to the hell of fire. So when you are offering your gift at the altar, if you remember that your brother or sister has something against you...

MARTYRS MIRROR
The Story of Fifteen Centuries of Christian Martyrdom from the Time of Christ to A.D. 1660
Thieleman J. van Braght

1530
Melchior Hoffman takes Anabaptism to the Netherlands

1533
Jacob Hutter becomes primary Anabaptist leader in Moravia

1534-35
Anabaptist revolution in Münster

1535
Phillipite Anabaptists fleeing Moravia are imprisoned in dungeon at Passau, and write hymns which are later included in the *Ausbund*

1536
Menno Simons leaves the established church to join the Anabaptists

1539
Anneken Jans drowned as an Anabaptist martyr

1565-95
Hutterite "Golden Age" in Moravia

1569
Dirk Willems turns back to save his pursuer, becomes martyr

1660
Thieleman J. van Braght publishes first edition of *Martyrs Mirror*

1693
Jakob Ammann leads movement among Swiss Anabaptists; his followers are known as Amish Mennonites

1700s
Swiss and German Anabaptists begin to immigrate to North America

1708
First Brethren baptism; Alexander Mack is the first Brethren minister

1870s
Mennonites from Russia begin immigration to North America

2000s
Anabaptists are a global fellowship, with congregations on all continents except Antarctica

1600   1700   1800   1900   2000

of the Anabaptist Story

Study Guide

Note: Some individuals using this guide may already be a member of, or participate in, an Anabaptist congregation. Others may not have much experience with an organized faith community. Adjust/choose questions as needed to fit your circumstances. Note also that many of the Discussion Questions and Extensions could apply to more than one chapter and a number of the Extensions could be stand-alone sessions.

INTRODUCTION

a) Write the word *Anabaptist* at the top of a large piece of chart paper. *What words, phrases, people, places, or faith practices come to mind when you hear the word Anabaptist?* Allow participants to think quietly for a few moments before answering. All responses should be accepted without judgment and written on the list. If not much is known or associated with the word, this can simply be acknowledged.

b) You may choose to make a similar list for "Mennonite," "Church of the Brethren," or another Anabaptist community. Save any lists made; it is interesting to look back at them after studying this material. You may, in fact, want to create new lists at the end of the series and compare the original and subsequent charts.

c) Journaling: Take time for individual reflection on any of the following prompts. Depending on time and comfort level, responses may or may not be shared with the group.
   i.   What is your faith background?
   ii. What about your current congregation is important to you?
   iii. What faith practices are meaningful to you?
   iv. If you have not been part of a congregation before, what is drawing you to that now?
   v.   What is something that puzzles you about church history, beliefs, or practices?

Chapter 1

<u>Discussion questions</u>

1) Regarding the practice of baptism:
   - What baptisms have you observed in your congregation?
   - In what other settings/churches have you witnessed baptisms?
   - Have you been baptized? If so, when and where? How did you reach that decision?
   - Are you considering baptism now? What questions do you have about baptism?

2) Can you be born an Anabaptist, or do you choose to be an Anabaptist? Can you be born a Mennonite, or do you choose to be Mennonite? Is this the same question, or two different questions?

3) How do lines between civil and religious authorities get blurred in today's world? What does it mean if a nation calls itself a "Christian nation"?

4) What movements are occurring in your congregation, conference, or community today?

5) Is it important to study Anabaptist beginnings? Why or why not?

<u>Extension</u>

a) Invite a pastor or adult congregation member to talk about his or her baptism experience. Questions for a visitor might include:
   - When were you baptized?
   - Where and how were you baptized? Who was present?
   - Why did you decide to be baptized?
   - Did you feel different after you were baptized?
   - How has baptism (and participation in a church community) affected your daily life?
   - What does baptism mean to you now? Has your understanding of baptism changed over the years in any way?
   - What advice or guidance would you give to someone who was considering baptism?

Chapter 2

Discussion Questions

1) Reading the Bible:
- When do you read the Bible?
- With whom do you read the Bible?
- What Bible translation do you have?
- How is the Bible a part of worship services in your church?

2) How are issues discussed and decisions made in your church or community today?

3) What issues were being discussed in the Zurich disputations between 1523 and 1525? What arguments could you make on behalf of Ulrich Zwingli? What arguments could you make on behalf of Conrad Grebel, Felix Mantz, and George Blaurock?

4) Do you know of any contemporary faith martyrs? How are people of diverse religious identities treated in your community today?

Extensions

a) Bring in several different Bible translations. Choose a scripture passage and compare.

b) Watch *The Radicals,* a 1990 Sisters and Brothers production. *The Radicals* tells the story of Michael and Margaret Sattler, two sixteenth-century Anabaptists.

Chapter 3

Discussion Questions

1) Regarding communion:
- How is communion shared in your congregation?
- What are different ways you have seen communion shared?
- What types of bread and juice/wine have you observed in communion services?

2) Regarding the Schleitheim Articles:
- What stands out to you? Why?
- Do any articles surprise you? If so, why?
- Are any of the practices listed visible in your congregation or community today?
- Some contemporary Anabaptists use Section VI of the Schleitheim Articles to say that the work of the military should be supported. An alternate understanding would be to consider this a statement of separation from society. What do you think?

Extension

a) Journaling: Take time for individual reflection on any of the following prompts. Depending on time and comfort level, responses may or may not be shared with the group.
  i. What from the first three chapters is significant to you?
  ii. What will you remember about these early Anabaptists?
  iii. What would you tell someone about how and why the Anabaptist movement started?
  iv. How does early Anabaptist history impact your understanding of church today?

Chapter 4

Discussion Questions

1) Consider the story of the *Stäbler* and the *Schwertler*. Does anything surprise you? What is memorable?

2) Consider the family and network of Archduke Ferdinand. Which of these individuals (for example: Charles V, Queen Isabel, Christopher Columbus) were familiar to you? In what contexts have you read or learned about them?

3) How does knowing the story of the Philippites affect how you read the words of the hymn "The Word of God Is Solid Ground" (lyrics on p. 35)?

Extensions

a) Arrange to sing "The Word of God Is Solid Ground" (*Mennonite Hymnal: A Worship Book* #314) in a worship service. Introduce the hymn to the congregation by telling the story of the Philippites.

b) Make a list of the ways in which your congregation or community shares resources. Is there a way to encourage or expand this practice?

Chapter 5

Note: When reading or telling the story of Münster, it may be helpful to create a list of characters/events as they appear in the narrative. Your list may look like this at the end:

- Melchior Hoffman
- Sikke Freerks Snijder
- *Stillstand*
- Jan Matthijs
- Bernhard Rothmann
- Bishop Franz Waldeck
- Jan van Leiden (King Jan)
- the cages at St. Lambert

Discussion Questions

1) What surprises you about the story of Münster? How do the actions of the Münsterite Anabaptists differ from what you would expect?

2) How do you think the events at Münster affected non-Anabaptists (common people, civil or religious authorities) in the region? How do you think the events at Münster affected Anabaptists in the region? How would you view the Anabaptist movement if the Münsterites were the only Anabaptists you knew?

3) What can be learned from the events at Münster? What should we carry forth from this story?

4) David Joris and Menno Simons were two Anabaptist leaders of the time who offered responses to Münster. Which of their positions (presented on p. 40) makes the most sense to you?

Chapter 6

Discussion Questions

1) How is Menno connected to the story of Münster, which is told in Chapter 5?

2) What were turning points in Menno's life?

3) Why was I Corinthians significant to Menno?

4) What do you think Menno would write about if he were alive today?

Extensions

a) Sing the hymn "O God, to Whom Then Shall I Turn" (as seen in sidebar on p. 46). The hymn is #61 in *Sing the Story* (Mennonite Publishing Network, 2007). How do these stanzas reflect Menno's life experiences?

b) Write the names of these groups of people on a chart.
•   Anabaptists
•   Common people
•   Magistrates
•   Learned scholars

Read aloud (or provide) the following Menno quotes for consideration. To whom was Menno directing his comments in each of the passages? (Page numbers refer to *The Complete Writings of Menno Simons*.)

i. "You must hearken to God above the emperor, and obey God's Word more than that of the emperor. If not, then you are the judges of whom it is written in Micah, They all lie in wait for blood; they hunt every man his brother with a net." (p. 204)

ii. "Your sacraments are an encouragement to the impenitent and your lives examples of wickedness...everywhere we find hatred, envy, hard and cruel hearts, a loathing aversion and disdain for the divine Word... You see, O barren trees and careless shepherds, these are the fruits you bring and the sheep you pasture." (p. 209)

iii. "Give ear, ye people, and lend the ear, all you who trust in lies and boast that you are Christians; tear your bands asunder and suffer yourselves no longer to be lead as asses bound under a heavy burden of sin by these aforementioned drivers, for they deceive you." (p. 212)

iv. "Fear not, little flock, for it is the Father's good pleasure to give you the kingdom. Not the perishing kingdom of Assyria, of the Medes, of Macedonia, nor of Rome, but the kingdom of the saints, the kingdom of the great King, of David, the kingdom of peace, of grace, and eternal peace, that shall never pass away but abide and stand forever." (p. 223)

[Answers: i. Magistrates, ii. Learned scholars, iii. Common people, iv. Anabaptists]

Chapter 7

Note: If possible, bring along a copy of *Martyrs Mirror* (perhaps borrowed from a congregation member or Mennonite institution, or purchased through Menno Media). It is also possible to view a copy online (options include mla. bethelks.edu/holdings/scans/martyrsmirror).

Discussion Questions

1) Are any of the *Martyrs Mirror* images familiar to you? Were any of the stories already known to you?

2) Are there reasons to tell or not to tell these martyr stories?

3) Are there places in the world today where people are martyred for their faith?

Extensions

a) Listen to *Singing at the Fire: Voices of Anabaptist Martyrs*, a 1998 recording of the Eastern Mennonite University Chamber Singers, under the direction of Kenneth Nafziger. This collection includes a hymn text based on the words of Menno Simons (see sidebar on p. 46).

b) Examine the Bearing Witness Stories Project website (www.martyrstories. org) to discover stories of contemporary, global Anabaptist faith witness.

c) Read selections from *Tongue Screws and Testimonies: Poems, Stories and Essays Inspired by the Martyrs Mirror* (sidebar, p.50). With which of the authors do you resonate? Are there authors who cause you to reconsider how you view or understand Martyrs Mirror?

d) Read the complete lyrics to Cruz Cordero's "Onward Martyrdom" in the July 2003 issue of Mennonite Historical Bulletin. See also cdero.workpress.com or the Mennonite Central Committee DVD Thermostat.

Chapter 8

Discussion Questions

1) What stories of women do you remember from previous chapters?

2) What leadership roles do women in your congregation or community have today? How are women visible in wider church structures (institutions, conference, or denominational positions) today?

Extensions

a) Invite a female pastor for conversation. Possible questions might include:
- When did you decide to become a pastor? Why?
- What was the path you took to prepare for pastoral leadership?
- What gifts do you bring to the pastorate?
- Who were your role models growing up? Who are they now?
- What do you enjoy most about being a pastor?
- What challenges do you face?
- Describe a typical week as a pastor.
- What advice would you give a person interested in becoming a pastor?

b) Journaling: Take time for individual reflection on any of the following prompts. Depending on time and comfort level, responses may or may not be shared with the group.

i. Consider an individual from Chapter 8 (*Martyrs Mirror*) or Chapter 9 (*Women of the Anabaptist Movement*). How are your faith and life experiences similar to that person? How are they different?

ii. What gifts do you have to offer your congregation or community?

iii. Who are your role models? Why?

Chapter 9

Discussion Questions

1) Reflect on stories from previous chapters. Which stories display violence? Which stories witness to a gospel of peace?

2) How does your congregation or community witness for peace? How can an individual share the peace of Christ with others?

3) What areas of the world today are experiencing violence in the form of wars? What forms of peace witness do you see in those areas?

4) In what ways is violence a part of North American society? What forms of peace witness are present?

5) What is a biblical foundation for nonviolence?

6) Consider the terms: *Nonresistance, nonviolence, nonviolent resistance, pacifism*. How are these terms related? How are they different? What individual or congregational actions would fit into these different categories?

Extensions

a) Identify a congregation or community member who has served as a CO. Invite that person to visit. Possible questions might include:

- What circumstances led you to be a CO?
- What was the process of becoming a CO?
- What support did you have? Did you face any adversity?

Certificate of Participation

_____
name

participated in a Christian Education series on Anabaptist history,
including sessions on the theology of nonviolence and conscientious objection
to military service. Anabaptists seek to follow the example of Jesus Christ.

Church: _____

Conference: _____

Date(s): _____

Teacher signatures: _____

**"See that none of you repays evil for evil,
but always seek to do good to one another and to all."**
(I Thessalonians 5:15)

**"The Prince of Peace is Jesus Christ… True Christians do not know vengeance.
They are the children of peace, and they walk in the way of peace."**
(Menno Simons, 1522)

- What was a typical day/week like?
- How has your CO experience shaped later job choices, thoughts, or interactions with others?

b) Identify a congregation or community member who has served with a service organization, such as those described on pages 68, 78, and 83. Invite that person to visit. Possible questions might include:
- How did you decide to become a volunteer with your organization?
- When, where, and for how long was your assignment?
- What was a typical day/week like?
- What was surprising about your experience? What was difficult about your experience? What did you enjoy most?
- How has your volunteer experience shaped later job choices, thoughts, or interactions with others?

c) Identify a peacemaker (Anabaptist, or otherwise-affiliated) in your area who is working for social, racial, or economic justice. Invite that person to visit. As a group, develop a list of questions prior to the visit. Consider in what ways you can get involved in this work.

d) Discuss the process of starting a Peace Portfolio for yourself. For specific guidance on what to include in a CO (or Peace) Portfolio, see www.centeronconscience.org. Consider including a copy of the Certificate of Participation provided in this Study Guide.

e) Engage in a Return to the Earth study group. Guides are available through Mennonite Central Committee (mcc.org/media/resources)

Chapter 10

Note: Each of the four main sections (Mennonites, Hutterites, Amish, Church of the Brethren) could be a session unto itself. If possible, invite congregation or community members (who represent the different Anabaptist branches) to join your discussions to share personal insights and stories.

HUTTERITES

Discussion Questions

1) What are the benefits of community living? What are the challenges?

2) In what ways are Hutterite communities of today similar or different from other contemporary Anabaptist groups?

Extension

a) Consider what you know about Jakob Hutter (see pp. 32-33), and then read these words of Jakob Hutter from 1535:

It is my heartfelt request to God that He will water His Garden with rain from Heaven, with the comfort of His Holy Spirit and the oil of His compassion. May He anoint all our hearts, pouring heavenly blessing upon His garden, so that it is fruitful and bears many good works. This garden is the Church of the living God. He raised a fence around His garden, to guard it from wild beasts. May He also protect it from bad thunderstorms and from evil blights so that the fruit may ripen, for the Lord's Eden is now in full bloom. May He himself keep watch over it and bring it to a bountiful harvest. (Haas, J. Craig. Readings from Mennonite Writings: New and Old. *Good Books, Intercourse, PA, 1992)*

AMISH

Discussion Questions

1) What practices/beliefs led Jakob Ammann to break away from other Swiss Anabaptists?

2) What are portrayals of Amish in the popular media? What is accurate? What might be incorrect?

Extension

If possible, find and listen to a recording of Amish singing. One option is *Amish Music Variety: From Harmonica to Hymns* available for purchase from various places. Recordings include hymns from the *Ausbund* (1997 Harmonies Workshop).

CHURCH OF THE BRETHREN

Discussion Questions

1) What were turning points in the life of Alexander Mack?

2) What is meant by "No creed but the Bible"?

Extensions

a) Read/sing "Move in Our Midst," #418 in *Hymnal: A Worship Book.* This is favorite Brethren hymn, often sung at annual gatherings.

b) If possible, have an individual of Brethren background talk to your group about the practice of footwashing. Consider planning a simple footwashing experience with your group or a larger congregational group.

c) Consider raising funds for a Heifer International project. Share *Faith the Cow* with the children of your congregation or community (sidebar, p. 77).

MENNONITES

Discussion Questions

1) Discuss the difference between Old Order and change-minded Mennonites. What are the strengths of each outlook? What are the challenges?

2) What is the history of Mennonites in your region? If you are part of a Mennonite congregation already, what is the history of your congregation?

3) In what ways are you connected to the Internet and social media? What benefits do you perceive? Are there dangers of which you should be aware?

Extensions

a) Look at recent copies of *Mennonite World Review* (MWR), or explore the MWR website. What topics are being discussed? What is the geographic span of the articles?

b) Look at recent copies of *Courier,* the Mennonite World Conference (MWC) newsletter, or explore the MWC website. What are the vision, mission, and shared convictions of MWC? Where and when will the next MWC Assembly be held? To what Anabaptist communities would you like to travel?

Summing Up

a) Look again at the lists you created at the beginning of the series. What new understandings have you gained? Consider making a new set of lists for the same words, or choosing new words (perhaps chapter titles) on which to reflect.

b) In what ways can you share new insights and information with members of your congregation or community?

c) Journaling: Take time for individual reflection on any of the following prompts. Depending on time and comfort level, responses may or may not be shared with the group.
  i.   What does it mean to explore the past?
 ii.   What does it mean to act in the present?
iii.   What does it mean to shape the future?

d) Arrange to visit/worship with other Anabaptist congregations in your area.

e) Visit an Anabaptist heritage center, museum, or library.

Resources

Ausbund, Das ist Etliche schöne Christliche Lieder, wie sie im dem Gefängniss zu Bassau in dem Schloss von der Schweizer Brüdern und von andern rechtglaubigen Christen hin and her gedichtet worden. Gale ECCO, 2010.

Beachy, Kirsten Eve, ed., *Tongue Screws and Testimonies.* Herald Press, 2010

Bender, Harold S. *The Anabaptist Vision.* Herald Press, 1944.

Bowman, Carl F. *Brethren Society: the Cultural Transformation of a "Peculiar People."* Johns Hopkins University Press, 1995.

The Complete Writings of Menno Simons, ed. by John C. Wenger. Herald Press, 1956.

Cordero, Cruz. "Onward Martyrdom" in *Mennonite Historical Bulletin,* July 2003.

Haas, J. Craig, ed. *Readings from Mennonite Writings, New and Old,* Good Books, 1992.

Hinz-Penner, Raylene. *Searching for Sacred Ground: The Journey of Chief Lawrence Hart, Mennonite.* Cascadia Publishing House, 2007.

Hoover, Susan Bame. *Faith the Cow.* Brethren Press, 1995.

Hymnal: A Worship Book. Faith and Life Press, 1992.

Klaassen, Walter and William Klassen, *Marpeck: A Life of Dissent and Conformity.* Herald Press, 2008.

Kraybill, Donald B., Karen M. Johnson-Weiner, and Steven M. Nolt. *The Amish.* Johns Hopkins University Press, 2013.

Landis, Susan Mark and Lisa J. Amstutz, eds. *Seasoned With Peace: Winter.* Peacemeal Press, 2010

The Mennonite Encyclopedia, Vol. 1-5. Mennonite Publishing House/Herald Press, 1955-1990.

The Mennonite Experience in America, vol. 1-4
MacMaster, Richard K. *Land, Piety, and Peoplehood: The Establishment of Mennonite Communities in America, 1683-1790.* Herald Press, 1984.
Schlabach, Theron F. *Peace, Faith, Nation: Mennonites and Amish in Nineteenth-Century America.* Herald Press, 1988.
Juhnke, James C. *Vision, Docrtine, War: Mennonite Identity and Organization in America, 1890-1930.* Herald Press, 1989.
Schlabach, Theron F. *Peace, Faith, Nation: Mennonites and Amish in Nineteenth-Century America.* Herald Press, 1988.
Toews, Paul. *Mennonites in American Society, 1930-1970: Modernity and the Persistence of Religious Community.* Herald Press, 1996.

Oyer, John S. and Robert S. Kreider. *Mirror of the Martyrs.* Good Books, 1990.

Packull, Werner O. *Hutterite Beginnings: Communitarian Experiments During the Reformation.* Johns Hopkins University Press, 1999.

Rideman, Peter. *Confession of Faith,* 2nd ed. Plough Publishing House, 1970.

The Schleitheim Confession, ed. by John Howard Yoder. Herald Press, 1977.

Scott, Stephen. *An Introduction to Old Order and Conservative Mennonite Groups.* Good Books, 1996.

Siegrist, Anne. "Immigrants Persist in Prayer, and Healing Follows." *Mennonite World Review,* November 24, 2014.

Sing the Story. Herald Press, 2007.

Snyder, C. Arnold and Linda A. Huebert Hecht, eds. *Profiles of Anabaptist Women: Sixteenth-Century Reforming Pioneers.* Wilfrid Laurier University Press, 1996.

van Braght, Thieleman J. *The Bloody Theater or Martyrs Mirror of the Defenseless Christians who baptized only upon confession of faith, and who suffered and died for the testimony of Jesus, their savior, from the time of Christ to the year A.D. 1660.* Herald Press, 1987.

Weaver, J. Denny. *Becoming Anabaptist: The Origin and Significance of Sixteenth-Century Anabaptism,* 2nd edition. Herald Press, 2005.

Media

The Radicals [DVD]. Vision Video, 2004

Singing at the Fire [CD]. Faith and Life Press

Thermostat: How Can We Turn Toward Peace in a Time of Fear? [DVD]. Mennonite Central Committee, 2005 (includes "Onward Martyrdom" by Cruz Cordero)

Websites

Bearing Witness (martyrstories.org)
Brethren in Christ [BiC] (bic-church.org)
Brethren Service Center.(brethren.org/brethrenservicecenter)
Christian Aid Ministries [CAM] (christianaidministries.org)
Church of the Brethren (brethren.org)
Christian Peacemaker Teams [CPT] (cpt.org)
Cordero, Cruz (cdero.workpress.com) Email: cdero2005@gmail.com
Global Anabaptist Mennonite Encyclopedia Online [GAMEO] (gameo.org)
Mennonite Central Committee (mcc.org)
Mennonite Church Canada (mennonitechurch.ca)
Mennonite Church USA (mennoniteusa.org)
Mennonite World Conference (mwc--cmm.org)
Mennonite World Review (mennoworld.org)

Note: The publisher and authors will gladly receive information that will enable them to rectify inadvertent omissions or errors in future editions.

Index

A patronymic is a name derived from an individual's father. In the Netherlands in the sixteenth century, it was commonplace for a person to be known by his or her own name, followed by his or her father's name. For example, the name Menno Simons means Menno, son of Simon. It is more accurate to refer to Menno Simons as Menno, rather than Simons. This is illustrated by the fact that Mennonites are not called "Simonites." In this index, the authors have chosen to connect page numbers to patronymics for individuals who were known in this way.

Credits and Permissions

for *Living the Anabaptist Story*
—David Rempel Smucker

Abbreviations:
C=credit; P=permission; t=top; r=right; l=left; b=bottom; m=middle.
First number left is page number. In a few instances, contact with the source or photographer was attempted but was not successful.

cover: CP, *Eradicating the Devil's Minions: Anabaptists and Witches in Reformation Europe, 1525-1600*, by Gary K. Waite. Toronto: Univ. of Toronto Press, 2007, p. betw. 160-61, from Hortensius, *Het boeck van den oproer*, Univ. of Amsterdam. Etching after painting by Barent Dirks, destroyed in 1652; design by Judith Rempel Smucker, Winnipeg, Man.
8: CP, David Rempel Smucker and Judith Rempel Smucker, Winnipeg, Man.
10-11: CP, authors.
12: C, "Karl der Grosse," *Wikipedia: Die Freie Enzyklopedia*, Daniel Baumgartner, 2005; P, Creative Commons Attribution ShareAlike 2.5.
13: C, "Martin Luther," *Wikipedia*, July 20, 2014, *A Question to a Mintmaker*, woodcut by Jörg Breu the Elder of Augsburg, ca. 1530; P, Creative Commons Attribution ShareAlike 2.5.
14t: C, "Martin Luther," *Wikipedia*, July 20, 2014. 1534 Luther Bible; P, Creative Commons Attribution ShareAlike 2.5.
14b: C, "Martin Luther," *Wikipedia*, July 20, 2014; both portraits of Luther and Katherine von Bora done by Lucas Cranach in 1528; P, Creative Commons Attribution Share Alike 2.5.
15: C, *Martyrs Mirror*, 1685, Book 2, p. 385; P, photo by Julie Kauffman, Muddy Creek Farm Library, Ephrata, Pa.
16: CP, *The German Peasants' War and Anabaptist Community of Goods*, by James M. Stayer, Montreal: McGill-Queen's Univ. Press, 1991, betw. x and xi, from Horst Buszello, *Der deutsche Bauernkrieg von 1525 als politische Bewegung* (Berlin: Colloquium, 1969), 152.

17: C, photo by George E. Bundy; P, Brethren in Christ Historical Library and Archives, Messiah College, Grantham, Pa.
18l: C, *Erstes Täufergesprach vom 17. Januar 1525. . .*, *from Abschrift zur bullingerschen Reformationschronik* von Heinrich Thomann, um 1605; P, Zentralbibliothek Zürich /Zürich Central Library, Zürich, Switzerland, Ms. B 316, fol. 182v.
18r: C, "Ulrich Zwingli," *Wikipedia: Die Freie Enzyklopedia,* painting by Hans Asper (1499-1571), Winterthur Kunstmuseum; P, Creative Commons Attribution Share Alike 2.5.
19: CP, Muddy Creek Farm Library, Ephrata, Pa., photo by Julie Kauffman.
20: C, "Desiderius Erasmus," *Wikipedia*, July 24, 2014; P, Creative Commons Attribution Generic license 1.0.
21: C, "Konrad Grebel," *Die Freie Enzyklopedia,* Gregor Helms/Gedenkstätten der Täuferbewegung; P, Creative Commons Attribution-Share Alike 3.0.
22l: CP, "The Radicals," www.theradicalsmovie.com.
22r: C, Georg Blaurock being whipped, from "Reformationsgeschichte," by Heinrich Bullinger, drawing by Ulrich Grob, *1618/1619;* P, Zentralbibliothek Zürich /Zürich Central Library, Zürich, Switzerland, Ms. L 61a, f. 429r.
23t: CP, "Amish Mennonite," by Doug Kaufman, Goshen, Ind., http://amishmennoniteineurope.blogspot.ca/2008/06/felix-manz-first-to-be-baptized-in.html
23b: C, *Ertränkung der Felix Manz in der Limmat/Drowning of Felix Manz in the Limmat, from Abschrift zur bullingerschen Reformationschronik von Heinrich Thomann, um 1605.;* P, Zentralbibliothek Zürich /Zürich Central Library, Zürich, Switzerland, Ms. B 316, f. 284v.
24: C, *Im rechten Bildteil entdecken obrigkeitlichen Truppen. . .zwischen Schlieren und Altstetten/*Discovery by Police Authorities. . . between Schlieren and Altstetten, *Sammlung Wickiana;* P, Zentralbibliothek Zürich, Zürich, Switzerland,

Ms. F23, p. 393-394.
25: CP, *Documents of Brotherly Love: Dutch Mennonite Aid to Swiss Anabaptists, Volume 1, 1635-1709,* translated by James W. Lowry. Millersburg, Ohio: Ohio Amish Library, 2007, p. 132.
26: C, "Schleitheimer Artikel," *Die Freie Wikipedia*, photo by Gregor Helms; P, Creative Commons Attribution /ShareAlike.
27t: CP, drawing by Ivan Moon; *Marpeck: A Life of Dissent and Conformity*, by Walter Klaassen and William Klassen. Scottdale, Pa.: Herald Press, 1989, cover.
27b: C, "Strasbourgh," *Wikipedia;* P, Creative Commons Attribution ShareAlike 3.00, photo by Jonathan Martz.
28t: CP, Bigstock photos.
28b: CP, *The Earth is the Lord's: A Narrative History of the Lancaster Mennonite Conference,* by John L. Ruth, p. 53, from *Mennonite Year Book and Almanac,* 1907.
29t: C, *Branch: A Memoir in Pictures,* by John L. Ruth. Lancaster, Pa. and Harleysville, Pa.: Tourmagination and Mennonite Historians of Eastern Pennsylvania, 2013, p. 343; P, Tourmagination, Waterloo, Ont.
29b: CP, Joanne H. Siegrist, Bird-in-Hand, Pa.
30: CP, David Rempel Smucker and Judith Rempel Smucker, Winnipeg, Man.
31: C, "Bathasar Hubmaier," *Wikipedia*, from H. J. Goertz, *Radikale Reformation*, München, 1978, portrait by Christophel van Sichem; P, Creative Commons Attribution ShareAlike 2.5.
32: CP, *Mennonite Attire Through Four Centuries,* by Melvin Gingerich. Breinigsville, Pa.: Pennsylvania German Society, 1970, p. 57, from *Gründliche kurtz verfaste Historia von Münsterischen Widertauffern: und wie die Hutterischen Brüder so auch billich, Widertauffer genet werden, im Lüblichen Marggrafffthumb Märhern, deren über die sibentzehen tausent sein sollen, gedachten Münsterischen in vilen ähnlich, gleichformig und mit zustimmet sein,* by Christopher Erhard. Munich: Adam Berg, 1588.
33: C, "Ferdinand I, Holy Roman Emperor," *Wikipedia;* P, Creative Commons Attribution ShareAlike 2.5.
34l: C, http://www.kelmscottbookshop.com/pictures/20524_2.jpg; P, Kelmscott Bookshop, Baltimore, Md.

34r: CP, *Mennonite Attire Through Four Centuries*, by Melvin Gingerich. Breinigsville, Pa.: Pennsylvania German Society, 1970, p. 88, from *Der Hutterischen Wiedertauffer Taubenkobel, in welchem all ihr Mist, Kot und Unflat . . . zu finden, auch des grossen Taubers, des Jakob Huters Leben . . .* Ingolstadt: Chr. A. Fischer, 1607.

35l: CP, *Hymnal: A Worship Book*. Scottdale, Pa.; Newton, Kans.; Elgin, Ill.: Mennonite Publishing House, Faith and Life Press, Brethren Press, 1992, no. 314.

35r: CP, David Rempel Smucker and Judith Rempel Smucker, Winnipeg, Man.

36: CP, Galen R. Frysinger, at http://www.galenfrysinger.com/germany_munster_saint_lambert.htm.

37: CP: *Menno Simons: Places, Portraits and Progeny*, by Piet Visser and Mary S. Sprunger. [English edition] Altona, Man.: Friesens, 1996, p. 21; also *Melchior Hoffman: Social Unrest and Apocalyptic Visions in the Age of the Reformation*, by Klaus Depperman. Edinburg: T & T Clark, 2000, frontispiece.

38t: CP, *Menno Simons: Places, Portraits and Progeny*, by Piet Visser and Mary S. Sprunger. [English edition] Altona, Man.: Friesens, 1996, p. 21.

38b: C, "Albion Cluny Medieval Sword," *Wikipedia*, CC-BY-2.0, by Soren Niedzilla; P, Creative Commons Attribution ShareAlike 2.0.

39t: CP, *Menno Simons: Places, Portraits and Progeny*, by Piet Visser and Mary S. Sprunger. [English edition] Altona, Man.: Friesens, 1996, p. 25.

39b, 40: CP, "Münster Rebellion," *Wikipedia*, *Historische Darstellung der Hinrichtung der Wiedertäufer auf dem Prinzipalmarkt von Münster, Westfalen, 1607, by Georg Berger, from Westfälische Kunststätten: Rathaus und Friedenssaal zu Münster*, seite 28.

41: CP, Galen R. Frysinger, at http://www.galenfrysinger.com/germany_munster_saint_lambert.htm.

42: CP, 2014 photo by Lyle Suderman, Winkler, Man. [at Winkler Bergthaler Mennonite Church, Winkler, Man.]

43+46: CP, *Menno Simons: Places, Portraits and Progeny*, by Piet Visser and Mary S. Sprunger [English edition] Altona, MB: Friesens, 1996, p. 98. Etching by Arend

Hendriks, from University Library, Mennonite Historical Library, Amsterdam, H 22.

44l: CP, *Menno Simons: Places, Portraits and Progeny*, by Piet Visser and Mary S. Sprunger [English edition] Altona, MB: Friesens, 1996, p. 65. Engraving by Christophel van Sichem, from F. W. H. Hollstein, *Dutch and Flemish etchings, engravings, and woodcuts, ca. 1450-1700*, Amsterdam, 1949, p. 37.

45t: C, http://pastorchuckwrbc.blogspot.ca/2012/07/pingjum-and-witmarsum-netherlands-july.html; P, Pastor Chuck McCullough, White Rock Baptist Church, Los Alamos, New Mex.

45b: CP, *The Complete Writings of Menno Simons*, ed. John Christian Wenger. Scottdale, Pa.: Herald Press, 1956.

47t: CP, 2014 photo by Lyle Suderman, Winkler, Man. [Winker Bergthaler Mennonite Church, Winkler, Man.]

47b: CP, photos by David Rempel Smucker and Judith Rempel Smucker, Winnipeg, Man.

48: C, 1685 *Martyrs Mirror*; P, photo by Julie Kauffman, Muddy Creek Farm Library, Ephrata, Pa.

49: C, *Martyrs Mirror*, Book 2, no. 812 [showing the Swiss Anabaptist Catherine Müller being led away from her child by the authorities]; P, Mennonite Library and Archives, Bethel College, North Newton, Kans.

50t: C, Top of the frontispiece of the 1685 *Martyrs Mirror*; P, Mennonite Library and Archives, Bethel College, North Newton, Kans.

50m: CP, *Menno Simons: Places, Portraits and Progeny*, by Piet Visser and Mary S. Sprunger [English edition] Altona, MB: Friesens, 1996, p. 135. From *Schriftuurlyke Geschiedenissen*, at University Library, Mennonite Historical Library, Amsterdam.

50b: C, cover of *Tongue Screws and Testimonies: Poems, Stories, and Testimonies Inspired by the Martyrs Mirror*, ed. Kirsten Beachy; P, Herald Press, Harrisonburg, Pa., 2010.

51: C, *Martyrs Mirror*, p. 980, 1886 English edition reprint; P, Mennonite Library and Archives, Bethel College, North Newton, Kans. has lower resolution at http://tools.bethelks.edu/mla/holdings/scans/martyrsmirror/ of 1685 edition,

Book 2, p. 661.

52t: C, *Martyrs Mirror*, Book 2, p. 65; P, Mennonite Library and Archives, Bethel College, North Newton, Kans.

52b: Mirror of the Martyrs exhibit is now at: C, Kauffman Museum, Bethel College, North Newton, Kans.; P, Martyrs Mirror Trust: Kauffman Museum, Bethel College, North Newton, Kans.; Mennonite Historical Library, Goshen College, Goshen, Ind.

53l: C, 1685 *Martyrs Mirror*; P, photo by Julie Kauffman, Muddy Creek Farm Library, Ephrata, Pa. [*Martyrs Mirror*, p. 741, 1886 English edition reprint; Bethel College website has high resolution at http://tools.bethelks.edu/mla/holdings/scans/martyrsmirror/ of 1685 edition, book 2, p. 387.]

53r: CP, Archives of the Mennonite Church USA, Goshen, Ind., EXL-008. [Laurie Oswald, "Passionate Resonance: Cruz Corderro meets Dirk Willems," *Mennonite Historical Bulletin* (July 2003): 8-10. This is part of a rap on Dirk Willems that he performed in Philadelphia in 2003 at the conference "Philadelphia Stories: Kingdom Building in the City."]

54: CP, photos by Judith Rempel Smucker, Winnipeg, Man. ["'Guns Into Plowshares' sculpture can be seen again—if you can find it, that is," *Washington Post*, by John Kelly, Jan. 17, 2011.]

55: C, Linda A. Huebert Hecht, *Women in Early Austrian Anabaptism, Their Days, Their Stories*, Kitchener, Ont.: Pandora Press, 2009, pp. 21, 221; P, Conrad Grebel University College, Milton Good Library, Waterloo, Ont.

56t: C, Linda A. Huebert Hecht, *Women in Early Austrian Anabaptism, Their Days, Their Stories*, Kitchener, Ont: Pandora Press, 2009, pp. 225, 239; P, Tourist Information Office of Aschau im Chiemgau, Germany [sketch by Philipp Apian from 1550, no. 9].

56b: C, "Augsburg," *Wikipedia*; P, Creative Commons Attribution ShareAlike, photo by Andreas Praefcke, 2006 [in Linda A. Hubert Hecht, Women in *Early Austrian Anabaptism, Their Days, Their Stories*, Kitchener, Ont.: Pandora Press, 2009, pp. 238, 240; from Kuntsammlung Stadt Augsburg, Augsburg, Germany, "Augsburger Perlachplatz im Winter, 1540, Nr. 9930," Heinrich Vogtherr the Younger.]

57: CP, "Burg Branzoll," *Wikipedia*, #mediaviewer/Datei:Burg_Branzoll_in_ Klausen.JPG, photo by Wolfgang Moroder.

58: C, *Martyrs Mirror*, Book 2, p. 209; P, Mennonite Library and Archives, Bethel College, North Newton, Kans.

59: C,"Mennonite Church USA Convention. . .,"*Mennonite World Review*, July 22, 2013; P, *Mennonite World Review*; photo by Jonathan Charles, Lancaster, Pa.

60: CP, Swarthmore College Peace Collection, Swarthmore, Pa., Charles Schumacher Collected Papers, 1930-2003, Collection CDG-A, photo by Ed Nazigun.

61: C, "Albion Cluny Medieval Sword," *Wikipedia*, CC-BY-2.0, by photo by Soren Niedzilla; P, Creative Commons Attribution ShareAlike 2.0.

62: CP, "Peace Be Still;" James He, Claremont, Cal. [www.heqiart.com].

63: CP, Freeman Network for Peace and Justice, Freeman, S.D.; artist Michelle Hofer; photo by Todd Jones.

64: CP, "A Short and Sincere Declaration," *Mennonite Historical Bulletin*, July 1974, p. 1.

65l: CP, Carl Bowman, *Brethren Society: The Cultural Transformation of a "Peculiar People,"* Baltimore: Johns Hopkins Press), p. 39. Brethren Historical Library and Archives, Elgin, Ill., from S. F. Sanger and D. Hays, *The Olive Branch of Peace and Good Will to Men*, 1907, p. 145.

65r: CP, Orie M. Conrad Collection, Mennonite Church USA Archives – Goshen, Ind.

66t: C, "Hutterite," *Wikipedia*, photo by I. Kleinsasser; P, Creative Commons Attribution ShareAlike 2.0.

66m: C, "Hutterite," *Wikipedia*; P, Creative Commons Attribution ShareAlike.

66b: C, "Alcatraz," *Wikipedia*; P, Creative Commons Attribution ShareAlike.

67t: CP, *Split Loyalties: Fraser Valley Mennonite Service in the Second World War*, by Michael Schmidt; University of Fraser Valley; at http://app.ufv.ca/fvhistory/students/wwII/ schmidtm/alternativeservice.html.

67b: CP, Mennonite Central Committee Photo Archives, Akron, Pa.

68tl: CP, "Sarah Thompson Appointed CPT Director," Christian Peacemaker Teams, www.cpt.org, Dec. 17, 2013.

68br, 68bl: CP, "Neighbors in Iraq," *The Mennonite*, May 1, 2010, pp. 20, 22, photos by Jamie Moffat.

69tl: CP, "Columbian Peace Group lends support. . .," *Courier/Correo/Courrier*, Oct. 2014, p. 1. hthttp://www.mwc-cmm.org/sites/default/ files/news_image_files/justapaz-web-edit. jpg.

69bl: CP, "Lawrence Hart's Visions of Peace," *The Mennonite*, Jan. 1, 2011, p. 16; photo by National Park Service.

69tr: CP, Mennonite Central Committee Photo Archives, Akron, Pa.

69 br: CP, photo by Mary Beyler, Obihiro, Japan.

70: CP, "Church Mission extends. . .," Mennonite Mission Network news, Aug. 5, 2010; http://www. mennonitemission.net/Stories/News/Pages/ Churchmissionincludessummercamp. aspx.

71: CP, Church of the Brethren, News Service, photo by Cheryl Brumbaugh-Cayford.

72: CP, Lenita Waldner, Silverwind Hutterite Colony, Man.

73t: CP, Lenita Waldner, Silverwind Hutterite Colony, Man.

73b: C, "Hutterite," *Wikipedia*, Martinsdale Hutterite Colony, Man.; P, Creative Commons Attribution ShareAlike 4.0 International.

74t: C, "Amish," *Wikipedia*; P, Ad Meskens, Creative Commons Attribution ShareAlike.

74b: CP, Bigstock photos.

75t: CP, Bigstock photos.

75b: C, "Amish Way of Life," *Wikipedia*; P, Creative Commons Attribution ShareAlike.

76t: C, "Alexander Mack," *Wikipedia* [seal of the Germantown Brethren congregation previously thought to be the personal seal of Alexander Mack because of the "A.M.," which more likely refers to "Abendmahl," the Brethren's Lord's Supper or Love Feast]; P, Creative Commons Attribution ShareAlike.

76m: C, "Alexander Mack," *Wikipedia*; P, Creative Commons Attribution ShareAlike.

77t: CP, Susan Hoover, *Faith the Cow*, illust. Maggie Sykora, Elgin, Ill., Brethren Press, 1995.

77m: CP, Brethren Historical Library and Archives, Elgin, Ill.

77b: CP, Church of the Brethren [www. brethren.org], News Service, Elgin, Ill., photo by Nathan and Jennifer Hosler.

78t: CP, Church of the Brethren [www. brethren.org], Service, photo by Jeanne Davies; http://www.brethren.org/ brethrenservicecenter.

78b: C, "An Amish Mennonite Family Album," by Tim Huber, *Mennonite World Review*, Mar. 18, 2013; P, photo by Everett Yoder [members and families at Calvary Christian Fellowship Mennonite Church gather outside their meetinghouse in Cottage Grove, Tennessee.]

79t: CP,"Beachy Amish Define Beliefs," by Tim Huber; *Mennonite World Review*, Apr. 16, 2014; [http://mennoworld.org/wp-content/ uploads/2014/02/beachy-singing2-web.png] [A worship service of a Beachy Amish group shows the plain clothing for men and women. Note the two styles of women's head coverings.]

79b: C, "The Beachy Amish Mennonites" http://www.beachyam.org/general.htm; General Information; P, Cory Anderson, Newcomerstown, Ohio.

80t: CP, Brenda Suderman [Home St. Mennonite Church, Winnipeg, Man.]

80lm: CP, "Church Planters Make Friends. . .," *Mennonite World Review*, Sept. 29, 2014.

80b: CP, Donita Wiebe-Neufeld, Edmonton, Alta.

81t: CP, "Black Mennonite Women Rock. . ." *Mennonite World Review*, Oct. 13, 2014.

81b: CP,"Immigrants Persist in Prayer. . ., "*Mennonite World Review,* Nov. 24, 2014, photo by Dan Gallagher.

82t: CP, "A Pieced Offering," *Mennonite Brethren Herald*, Nov. 2013, p. 7.

82b: CP, Bigstock photos.

83t: CP, Mennonite Disaster Service, Lititz, Pa.

83b: C, "Global Youth Summit to precede 2015 PA conference," *Courier/Correo/ Courrier*, Dec. 2014, p. 3; P, Mennonite World Conference.

84-85: map and design by Judith Rempel Smucker, Winnipeg, Man.

86-87: content by authors; images from prior pages, Bigstock photos.

Acknowledgements

Our deepest thanks go to Judith Rempel Smucker and David J. Rempel Smucker, who worked hours upon hours on image gathering, permissions, and layout design. This book would not exist without you. *Go Team Winnipeg!*

To the Fransen Family Foundation, we offer our sincere appreciation for the financial support which made this endeavor possible. Blessings as you continue to support projects throughout the global Anabaptist community.

Recognition goes to our home congregation of Madison Mennonite Church (Madison, Wisconsin). In particular, thank you to the high school youth of Madison Mennonite, who have participated in Sunday School classes and discussion groups using this material. Your comments and questions shaped this book.

In addition to the individuals identified in the captions, photos, photo credits, and resource list, we would like to thank Ron Adams, Lorraine Stutzman Amstutz, Mary Beyler, Cheryl Brumbaugh-Cayford, Brenda Burkholder, Hedda Durnbaugh, Paul Durnbaugh, Jonathan Dyck, Megan Fazio, Leonard Gross, Mona Jean Harley, Linda Huebert Hecht, Deb Hoffman, Susan Horein, Don Kraybill, Gerald Mast, Steve Nolt, Dave Mauer, Colleen McFarland, Titus Peachey, John D. Roth, Joe Springer, Henry VanderHill, Jon VanderHill, Mary Weaver, Seth Weaver, Tonya Ramer Wenger, Earl Zimmerman, and the many additional people who responded enthusiastically when we answered the query, "So, what are you working on right now?"

Finally, thank you to Michael A. King of Cascadia Publishing House LLC. Your knowledge, expertise, and editorial guidance is of great value.

—Lisa Weaver, J. Denny Weaver

PHOTO BY KENT SWEITZER